Tennis Strategies

And

Other Revelations

That Dumbfounded Me

When I Finished the Tour

Barbie Bramblett

Tennis Strategies and Other Revelations
That Dumbfounded Me When I Finished the Tour

Copyright © 2013 by Barbara Christine Bramblett

ISBN 978-0-615-75611-0

Printed in USA by 48HrBooks (www.48HrBooks.com)

First Paperback Edition

Written and Edited by Barbara Christine Bramblett

This book is dedicated to

all people who love the game of tennis.

Acknowledgments

I am very grateful to my parents, Norman and Marie, and my sister, Michelle, for the strong support that I have received regarding my life's pursuits. I extend a special thanks to the many people who have been close friends throughout my life, and those who were instrumental and inspirational during my tennis playing career including Jim Parker, Adrian Bey, Harry Drummond, Eve Schwartz and thousands of men, women and children who I have taught tennis lessons to over the years.

EVERY APPROACH IN THIS BOOK

IS EQUALLY APPLICABLE

TO ALL

SINGLES & DOUBLES PLAYERS

(unless otherwise specified)

Contents

CONTENTS

CONTENTS

3 THE VISUAL APPROACH

4 INTENSIFYING TOURNAMENT & LEAGUE PLAY

CONTENTS

It has been my experience that attempting to alter and enhance a player's technique to strike the ball does not prompt a player to win more often.

Rather, it's understanding the full scope of the game, how to win and what is necessary to win that leads players to naturally advance.

Barbie

Tennis Strategies

And

Other Revelations

That Dumbfounded Me

When I Finished the Tour

RELAX, GET COMFORTABLE AND ENJOY THE READING

My delightful intention wishes to share with you a voluminous understanding of 21st century tennis. The succinct knowledge in this book promises to endow your winning tennis game with discovery, instant improvement and creativity. This material has been written for players who love tennis yet lack the luxury of time to construe its scientific framework.

I wish that this information and wisdom I impart to you could have been conveyed to me in the earliest stages of my tennis career. My professional tennis experience and post-tour analytical study is my contribution to you. Tennis is opulently abstract, hypnotically appealing, and sublimely visceral. As a result, a player's perceptions are sometimes counter-intuitive, since the enigmatic charm of tennis is tiered with overlapping dimensions and comprehensive themes.

Both singles and doubles players will benefit immensely from a plentiful understanding of the court and the newest methods recently surfacing from the original stratum of the sport. Earlier instruction was infamous for presenting step-by-step deliberations. But today's tennis has been swooped into an innovative flow where novel racquet technology and illumined modern tactics transport the game to fresh levels.

Up-to-date approaches and strategies have made the former methodology more apparent. I clarify the importance of those authoritative features for winning, which debunk the popularized myth of constructing points. Balls travelling with piercing velocity combine with the latest strategies to create a commanding and impenetrable game structure. An invention of unique shots has been born along these contemporary lines of tennis. Therefore, this book offers you a clear-cut approach recognizing the rapid change.

The assembled writing is organized into concise sections with 5 complementary chapters. Each part provides you with a tennis specialty. The strategy is explained through the forms of tactics, conversational objectives, techniques, mental aspects, diagrams and hundreds of tips for your tennis insight, which ultimately guide to sharpen your advancement. Too often in my many years of teaching tennis, I have roamed the courts and I've seen dedicated players trying hard to win though those players, unbeknownst to them, were uninformed about how to use the entire court.

One of the reasons tennis players choose this sport is to display their creativity and instinctive competitiveness. You are the stars for you comprise the special group of players with passion for tennis. Your competitors may be neighbors, friends, new acquaintances or business colleagues. Or, you might play recreational tournaments, club leagues or share tennis get-togethers whilst basking in the pleasure of this exciting game.

By the time you finish reading this book, you will be able to comprehend exactly what occurs in a match and why. With this realization, you will be eager to embark upon your creative tennis quest. Whether you are a daily recreational player, a highly competitive junior, a singles or doubles player, an avid tennis reader, a weekender, a bystander, a beginner or even aspiring to be on the tour, your tennis perspective will soon be decidedly broadened by this learning experience.

I hope that you enjoy the reading and I am most certain that your skills and perspectives will instantaneously improve as you add these bold concepts to your tennis game of the new millennium.

1

A MAESTRO OF BALANCE

Let's begin. The foremost objective is to transform your tennis outlook by standing in the shoes of the tallest tennis player that has ever existed. Although this analogy may sound simplistic, you will gain fresh knowledge with a new view. If you might take just one moment to inquire into this analogy, the reasoning will improve your tennis game instantly.

At towering heights, you sustain broadened court vision. One of the most detrimental effects that a player generates in competition occurs when the head moves around too much. A player's vision will inconsistently move through various levels of space. Precision is hard to come by when vision bee bops all over the court.

A golden aspect found in a professional touring player is the stillness of the head throughout a ball strike. Players should be aware that when the chin moves up and down, so does the head which supports the vision. Players need to keep their heads as still as possible to avoid shifting their vision. The head should be compliantly balanced during a player's movements. Eyesight and perception should be composed and unfettered.

The standard tennis technique has changed because a player's natural predisposition to strike the ball now prevails. Players who want to further improve their ball strikes should spartanly focus on their tennis postures. When the chest is open and the shoulders are pulled back, the head is naturally balanced. Breathing can be easily affected unless the torso is upright. All body parts work together in sync instead of jostling with one another.

ENLIGHTENMENT ONE

The Prize is Wide-Ranging Vision

Cultivate pristine balance
to view the court area
as the tallest player would perceive it

Refrain from slouching

Keep the chin raised and level

Breathe fully

HOW HARD SHALL I CRUNCH THE BALL?

The story about the time element in tennis must be told. In the past, the game displayed long rallies and designed plays. Today, players need to constantly catch their balance, ready to react. Players are reactive, instead of thinking or planning a series of shots to strike next. The accelerated speed of the ball flight has forced players onto a path of relentless recovery.

In an idealized version, a player would cover immense distance and would be perfectly balanced before and after the strike. Certainly, singles and doubles players should aspire to arrive to the ball early to reap additional preparation time. But more significantly, balance reveals the importance of the body's resurgence *after* the shot has been hit. Players must attempt to regain their physical stability and strength after striking their shots. This element has been intensified in today's tennis. Days of planning a sequence of groundstrokes disappeared decades ago because time is scarce.

A tennis player should avoid striking the ball mindlessly to the other side of the net with all of one's raw power. This hurls a loss of control, creates unsteady balance and throws vision to the breeze. What appeared to be a paramount shot returns abruptly and boomerangs back into the court, leaving a player wavering and unguarded. When this happens, the player has lost precious time that could have been resourcefully used for recovery.

Poignantly expressed, your fast-striking swings without a time designated strategy frequently place you on "the defense."

Yes, you witness the televised touring players pummel the tar out of the ball. You will arrive at that element in the near future. You, too, shall produce power-loaded shots at the appropriate time. But your primary powers of control must first be acknowledged, distinguished and defined at this strategic stage before attempting to successfully implement fierce force into your game.

ENLIGHTENMENT TWO

Time, Bona Fide Power, Command

The faster you strike the ball like bursting from a
canon,
the faster the ball returns to you
leaving you meager time for recovery
limiting your balance and accuracy

Bona fide power is also defined as
the skill of finesse, intelligence
out-smarting the opponent
attaining command
athletic proficiency
sharp vision
precision

HOW MANY STEPS DO I REALLY NEED TO TAKE?

Tennis players are often led to improve incrementally from instructional rhetoric instead of first led to understand the all-encompassing concept. When you have received instruction, do you recall someone convey that you needed to run faster and anticipate? This brusque information was supplemental yet it neglected to emphasize *why* your agile footsteps support your tennis play.

Scuttling and scurrying with as many steps as you can possibly formulate achieves easy-reaching, magnificent court coverage. However, court speed is more than quickly peddling footsteps. In all likelihood, a tennis player will never be able to claim superb reach on every shot. The court area from the right-alley sideline to left-alley sideline and from the baseline to the net is vast and roomy. Nevertheless, the court should be covered as swiftly and smoothly as possible.

Court speed is entwined with tactical attributes such as balance and good vision. Court speed is also coupled with buying time and knowing how to read an opponent's shots from their departure points. Enhancing your speed on the court compliments your potential tennis adroitness. The mélange of physical balance, time, power, command and ideal vision is in unison with foot-speed. This combination is the reason why you should be quick on your feet.

True Swiftness

It matters little to run fast like a cheetah
if a player is unaware of the grander purpose

Wide-ranging vision
balance
bona fide power
and
precisely reading
your opponents' departing shots
are
objectives
behind quickened foot speed

Anticipation will lead to your tennis ingenuity

REALLY, IT'S A BIG SPACIOUS COURT!

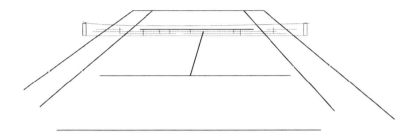

The biggest misconception which many players have about their own games is the belief that the majority of their errors sail "out." Ask thousands of tennis players where they suppose their mistakes are made and they will articulate; "I strike the ball way out of the court. Hitting out is easy for me. I seldom ever strike a ball into the net." Players assume that striking the ball into the net is respectable and acceptable. Consequently, those netter mistakes rarely make a memorable dent. This theme is accountable for singles and doubles players' games attaining a certain level and then reaching a plateau. Ah, the perceptions we believe contrasted to the realities of truth! This major matter will be explored more extensively in the following chapters.

In actuality, the tennis court is an elongated spacious playground where players divulge their most creative choices. Many players may view a shortened, abbreviated court which influences a player's shot-making dexterity. This picturesque outlook leads some tennis players to observe the service boxes, no man's land and the baseline on the other side of the net all at once through the rope cords, underneath the net tape. A subconscious inclination silently summons players to strike balls into that area viewed underneath the tape. The service boxes appear to players as wide squares, contrary to their rectangular shapes. Furthermore, no man's land appears closer than it is.

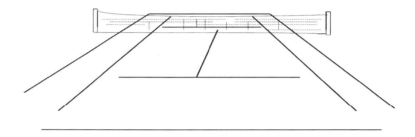

Players remain fully cognizant that their ball strikes must inevitably travel over the net tape. Yet, here resides the spatial dilemma that tricks a player's perception regarding the real dimensions of the tennis court. A player's vision fathoms one picture, *viewing the court underneath the net tape* through the rope cords. But rationally and consciously, players' superfluous maneuvers strike to send the ball *over the net* to the other side. This push and pull predicament, this tug of war felt deep within a tennis player's consciousness which pertains to the ball flight and destination, has players habitually pegging the net. This mysterious affair continues to stump players' abilities albeit until the optical illusion of the court's complexion is dismantled and revealed in its entirety.

The Splendor of Space

You will acquire a new sense of the court
as you discover
the area across the net
is larger than you perceive

Be clever and avoid striking in the net

The beauty of tennis lays in your creativity,
imagination and invention

The Bottom Line Isn't the Baseline

Instructional technique on serves and return-of-serves are learned after a player strikes the ball proficiently and has played for a comfortable period of time. Nevertheless, the serve and return-of-serve are seldom given the whopping attention they deserve. The bottom line is that these shots contain the largest command and the finest strategy. The assumption that the serve and the return are used to initiate the ball into play is alarming. To curtail the emphasis on the serves and the returns discounts a tennis player's strategic strengths.

The serve and the return-of-serve are the most eminent components of your tennis game. These two features highly determine the outcome of your matches. Why do singles and doubles players spend so much time on other aspects of their games instead of enhancing their quintessential service and return-of-serve skills necessary to win more frequently? With strengths like these, the match could be halfway or completely won. The serve and the return-of-serve are the very first shots that you place into the court.

Once the calculated odds are understood regarding the serve, return-of-serve and the court's spaciousness, players will compliment their games with originality. A player will invent shots as a resulting reaction from the fast pace of exchange. However, a player's reactive invention of shots is conspicuously different from setting out to intentionally construct a sequenced shot progression within the point. Singles and doubles tennis players who invent plays are being naturally creative in the spur of the moment, as opposed to the idea of constructing a point which implies a manageable building from one shot to the next.

The serve and the return-of-serve are the main builders of the point. All other counteractions reactively follow the lead of those 2 preceding shots. To construct a point suggests that players have unlimited time to plan and formulate a string of related shots. In some ways, constructing a point might be trying to propose the image of pounding away, aggressively running an opponent until the point is won. But players rarely rely on their controlled, lithe construction, players rely on their spontaneous aggression. The intention is about dominance and command. Today, players are dealt little time for scrutinized analysis during a flurry of shot exchange. Hence, all league players, weekenders, touring players, juniors and recreational competitors must create what they find possible within the seconds of a point.

It's About Serve and Return

The crux of the matter rests on the serve
and the return-of-serve

Make a special effort to develop
the strongest serves and return-of-serves

Know how critical serves and return-of-serves
are for winning matches

2

A MAGNIFYING GLASS

A description of the number of bare minimum points needed to win a match is critical information for singles and doubles players. To fully grasp the impact of tennis scoring, a systematic analysis of points must be rendered. Understanding the influence of scoring in its simplicity will enable players to comprehend the match in its complexity. This straightforward analysis will display a chart for quick assimilation.

Players must immediately be cognizant upon inquiry that 24 points will occur in a set regardless of their circumstances. Singles and doubles players must know this specific amount of minimum points played in one set at the snap of their fingers. Identifying these points magnifies the significance of the vital points necessary to win a match.

Ask any tennis player, "How many points do you need minimum to win one set?" and an expeditious answer should be expected: "24 points." If a player needs to take a moment to recognize the minimum number of points per game, 4 points multiplied by 6 games equals 24 points, it reveals a player's unfamiliarity over the mammoth character that these points possess. Why consign flippant emphasis to these trifle points? This question solicits the secret to playing assertive tennis.

This chart illustrates the number of minimum points needed to win each set in singles or doubles.

Minimum Points to Win a Match

1st Set	2nd Set
6-0	6-0
24 points minimum	24 points minimum

How many points, minimum, are required to win an entire match without losing one point? 48! Players need this information to be topmost in their thoughts. This perspective of guaranteed points lays at the core of a player's tennis strength. The x-ray of the scoring apparatus is absolutely imperative to know. This tool will enlighten your perspective and renovate your manner of play.

Only 48?

"48 points" regally declares that a player (or team) wins each point, never loses a point and wins each and every point consecutively. This hypothetical example is the most simplified paradigm leading you to comprehend the critical roles of the serves and the return-of-serves. As the reader you probably howl, "Sounds wonderful, 48 points, but that's IMPOSSIBLE to do." Yes, what you believe may be true, however you will derive wisdom to take full advantage of your own serves and return-of-serves. The purpose of this clear-cut study reveals the ascendancy you maintain with these shots.

When players begin a match, in general, they get ready to face the unknown, point by point, and think step-by-step. Nonetheless, if players enter the unknown realizing that they need at least 48 points to win the match, their approach is more defined. Players are guaranteed 24 points to serve and 24 points to return serve. Consequently, these players should want their serves and return-of-serves to be their best pitches. (Players are actually allotted 48 serves minimum, including 1st and 2nd serves). Understanding how these vital points stride through the sets probably seems irrelevant until players realize their budding potential to take charge.

You want to be dominant from the beginning of each point, whether it's with your serve or your return-of-serve. Your serve is the first ball you initiate the point with, the very first ball you will place into the court. When given that auspicious opportunity in tennis, you must take full advantage of it. The return-of-serve is also the first ball that *you* have a chance to place into the court. Although your return-of-serves offer less assurance for winning points than serves, when granted the commanding opportunity to begin the point, you must tackle the returns regardless of the resistance.

The groundwork of the serve and the return-of-serve, those first two shots that a player strikes, dictates what type of point a player will play. Shall players be in charge of the point, dominate, be in control, be offensive or sashay the control to their opponents? The serve and the return-of-serve are the most critical, focal shots that a tennis player executes when playing a match. The precedent reveals your serves and your return-of-serves are the first balls that *you* strike into the court. Your serves and return-of-serves decisively set you up from the beginning to win the point or lose the point. That's why each point minimally allotted to each game holds so much weight and consequence!

Let's imagine that you have won the majority of your service games so you have just about won every other game. Although this hypothetical ideal is an example, it reveals that you have practically won half of your match. Obviously, players would love if their matches neatly transpired as in the case just mentioned. Both singles and doubles tennis players must know that their service games are the ones they must ambitiously conquer.

Players should view their return-of-serve games with a similar analogy. Let's say that you decide to drastically improve your return-of-serves. If your return-of-serves are strong, you could lead with a superb advantage when your opponent is serving. Needless to say, it's illogical to conceive a tennis player wins every game played but understanding the imperative role that serves and return-of-serves uphold sets you up to grasp tennis' powerful strategy.

The reality is that you will play more than 48 points in a match. But half of that match, half of the sum of all points, you will begin the point from scratch. An explanation of a common example of scoring is complimented with a chart (on page 41); *A Hypothetical Match With Scoring*. This scoring can be applied equally to singles and doubles players. This example is simple and very realistic.

The purpose of this example is to display the basic design of a match. This reveals how often you are guaranteed serves and return-of-serves, pointing to *how significant* those first shots are.

Let's imagine at the conclusion of your match, the final score turned out to be 6-4, 7-5 (regardless if you won or lost). Add all the games together and you find that 22 games were played in total.

For this example, imagine that 10 points were played in each game. Consequently, each game arrived to deuce. Each game went deuce, ad-in, deuce, then ad-out and finally you or your opponent won the game. In an actual match, anywhere from 4 to 15 points can be a common number of points played in a game.

If 22 games were played and 10 were points played per game, this totals 220 points played in this match.

You served 110 points. So, you had 110 chances to take command of the point, actually 220 opportunities when you include your 2nd serves! You also had 110 chances to return serve!

Here's a tie-breaker example. In a tiebreaker, you (as a singles player) serve every 2 points and return the serve every 2 points. Since a doubles team alternates serving and returning every 2 points, it signifies that doubles partners should have strong serves and return-of-serves! As a singles player or a doubles team, you can easily win the majority of points in the tiebreaker initiated from your strong serves and your strong return-of-serves. In these circumstances, it's highly predictable that your team will win the set.

The incongruities of tennis may appear enigmatic, yet the game is completely decipherable when players realize the magnitude their serve and return-of-serve control. Recognizing this information should lead players to pay strong attention to their serve and return especially above any other part of their games that they could ever have imagined eminent.

A Hypothetical Match With Scoring

Final Score: 6-4, 7-5

Total Games Played: 22

10 points were played in each game:

22 Games x 10 Points per game

= 220 Total Points

You Served 110 points

You Returned (Return-of-Serves) 110 points

The next sections further elaborate on strengthening significant aspects of your serves and return-of-serves so they decisively influence your match play.

THE SERVE

If you have come to an agreement about your tennis serve's potential, you might find yourself reminiscing in reverie, visualizing the new serve which you are preparing to develop, to strike into the court from towering heights. Only in extracting the opportune consequences from service situations do tennis players recognize the modus operandi at play.

First, emulate the attributes of the tallest tennis player by elevating your posture. Focus your sights higher over the net instead of simply viewing the service box. You are given the navigational choice to place your serves on the right-hand side of the service box, the left side or through the middle. And you are given an even bigger choice, to make sure that your serves evade soaring into the net! The star-spangled idea is to send the serve into the court more vertical and less horizontal. In a hypothetical version, your serve would bounce high, landing deeply into your opponent's court never to be returned. Since your serves will return to you upon ostensible occasion, you should concentrate on serving 2-4 feet over the net to create a similar effect, rather than skimming the net by a few inches.

Serving with height over the net accomplishes 2 feats: 1) it pushes your opponents further back during their return-of-serve exploits and 2) the added service height prevents your ball from pegging the net with errors. This exclusive plea begs no errors are flung into the net. Serves traveling too near to the net chronically sail into the net.

Serves

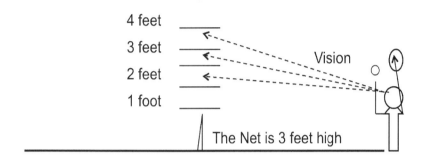

Servers should also focus their vision
2, 3 and 4 feet *above the net* before they serve,
instead of only looking at the service boxes.

When dispatched as heavily hit topspin serves, players' imposing serves will bound near opponents' heads. Instead of developing such an arsenal at this juncture, attempt to imitate the serve's flinging effects. Aim into the court from the highest point above your head. Your serves will spring further into the service boxes with force.

Many players erroneously assume when witnessing their serves strike the net tape, their attempts were on the verge of success. This unfortunate happenstance reveals the contrary. If a serve sails into the net, even if the serve travels over the net, that ball is likely to land "short" within the service box. Soaring low over the net invites a poor and inconsistent outcome. The strongest shot in the program - the serve - you surely would never want it to bring down your results. Intelligent players cringe when their serves peg the net. These players also realize that serves will be missed and if so, it's better that they fly out. Having the liberty to swing much higher over the net, utilizing the deeper portions of the service box makes the serve twice as effective.

The Serve vs. The Groundstroke

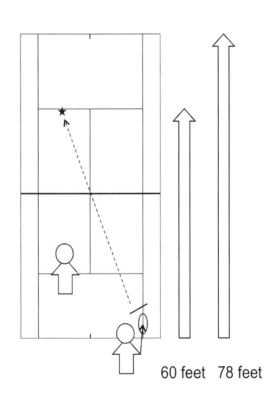

The potential for service travel is only 18 feet less than a groundstroke which lands on the baseline.

60 feet   78 feet

Singles and doubles tennis players must focus on the weaker sides of their opponents' return. An astute server would never unfurl freebees at an expense of a few supersonic serves that serendipitously dip into the court once in a while. A double fault handed to an opponent is an opponent's unearned gift. A player must prevent this double-faulting impasse.

Everyone finds it more pleasant to discuss how tennis players win sets rather than how sets are lost. However, this next evaluation exposes the reality of the situation. You have only 2 tries per service box. Take your time. You need a clear intent to place your 1st serve inside the box. A player should avoid having to depend on that 2nd serve. What if that 2nd serve is haphazardly missed? 4 double faults within a set is a glowing donation equivalent to an entire game!

Let's differently rearrange the loss of these "4" double-faulting points distributed within the set. Imagine the score is 5-5 in the set and deuce. Your opponent needs only 2 points to forge ahead, 6-5. Now the score is 6-5. You arrive at deuce once again and your opponent only needs 2 points to win this next game. Winning those 2 points, your opponent completes and wins the set 7-5. The meaning of this tale is that a player is at the mercy of losing by 2 points at 5-5, deuce, and 2 more points at 6-5, deuce. Four points can dispense the set to an opponent. A frivolous subtraction of four points can slip from a player's control, handing the set to an opponent on a silver platter.

Why pound away at four double-faulting points that occurred earlier in the set? Those double faults could have been dodged at these important stages, 5-5 or 6-5 in the set. But the sum of four double-faulting points ultimately balanced out the total of points to create the present situation. A completed set without those incidental double faults would have positioned the player ahead in the number count by four extra points. Instead, those double faults placed a player at the mercy of the score. The spare points could have changed the whole outcome of the set.

You might believe that you would never issue this many double faults in a match and one would hope this is true. Let's bend and stretch this example just a bit, replacing those double faults with 2nd serves. A player who relies on 2nd serves has been put into a similar defensive situation. Weak 2nd serves jilt a player's chances to win the requisite service points.

This summative strategy deems that double faults can be evaded if players *focus* on placing 100% of their 1st serves inside the court. A commanding play will ensue without riskily relying on second serves as backup. A player's consistent deep first serves prepared in practice and match play are analogous to submitting a grandiose serve that never returns.

A tennis player's game is molded by its comprehensive methodology. Thus, players will perform in their future matches similar to the way they play their present ones. In fact, singles and doubles players might be surprised to find their matches will be almost identical in stats to their previous matches unless an extra effort is made to change.

The Path of Good Vision

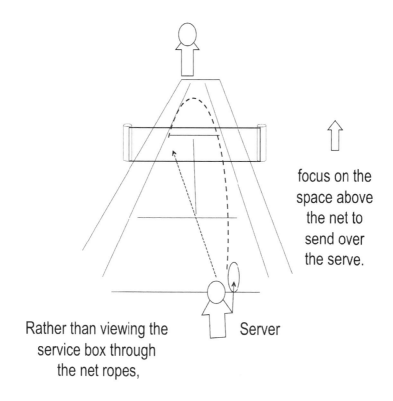

focus on the space above the net to send over the serve.

Server

Rather than viewing the service box through the net ropes,

THE RETURN-OF-SERVE

A peculiar paradox resides over the return-of-serve skill because most tennis players are inattentive to the shot. But the return-of-serve is the second most critical shot a player needs. Players who win all their service games and in tandem break the opponent's service game once throughout each set will triumph and win the match. Breaking an opponent's service game is considered at times a troublesome and difficult feat. A player's successful return can largely depend on the strengths or weaknesses of an opponent's serve. Nevertheless, creating errorless return-of-serves should be a primary goal.

Recall times when you have practiced, competed, drilled or even taken a tennis lesson. You probably devoted 10 or 15 minutes toward the end of the session to practice serves with meager moments leftover for focusing on return-of-serve skills. And your return-of-serves skills exemplify the other half of your tennis strength! Do you remember warm-up situations before a match began where you indifferently drove back a few return-of-serves? Automatically receiving your opponents' serves while warming up, you had the opportunity to pay close attention to the serves' trajectory. Many practice and warm-ups sessions prior to matches have left the return-of-serves in the trenches, believing those returns will take care of themselves when the match begins. These claims illustrate a crystal clear picture why your game instantly improves when you focus on your return-of-serves.

Rallies and volleys are unequal to the tactical importance of the return-of-serve. Although this return is created with a groundstroke, it arcs differently from a normal groundstroke. Whereas groundstroke rallies are received on a level plane, the returner receives serves that spring upward after landing. The serve's trajectory bounces toward the returner more assertively than a groundstroke. The serve approaches the court from a higher plane, reflecting and relating to the server's height and extensive reach. Strangely enough, the serve is, in actuality, a short shot. The serve arrives into the service box, landing short within the full-sized court since the service line is nearly halfway inside the court.

The returner must manage a ball that arrives short in the court, is more dynamic than a groundstroke, veers sharply and depends on the server's extended service height. Often, the returner must strike the ball to pull it downward from the bounce's trajectory. Fortunately, the returner is exempt from having to run side-to-side in retrieval. Outfitted with this data, returners should consider ahead of time the general vicinity of the bounce.

Effective ideas for improving and developing strong return-of-serves are listed in the next section, *Top 10 Tactics for Return-of-Serve*.

Top 10 Tactics for Return-of-Serve

1. Anticipation

Players must take into account the targeted area where the server's ball will reliably land 80%-90% of the time. A returner experiences an intimidating spatial image while preparing to receive serve, assuming that the entire service box must be visually covered instead of a distinct region. Serves generally land a few feet from the service line, sideline or midline. This indicates that serves rarely land 3, 4 or even 8 feet from the net. The returner should prepare to receive and strike the ball from an already specified area of the court since servers almost never utilize the totality of service box space. Contrary to sheer guessing, the returner should be aware of the probability where their returns will most likely be struck.

A spin serve, which may land shorter than expected, slightly changes the returner's anticipatory situation. The short spin serve pegs the sideline and veers off the court with more verve than a regular serve, defying predictable regions that are used inside the service box. Spin serves must be recognized early to certify whether the server possesses these atypical twisting serves. If the server does not use a spin serve, returners are free of angst and lack worry of being swooshed off the court.

Service Box Anticipation

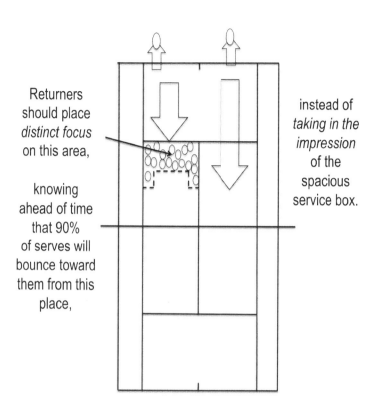

Returners should place *distinct focus* on this area,

knowing ahead of time that 90% of serves will bounce toward them from this place,

instead of *taking in the impression* of the spacious service box.

Cutting Off The Angle

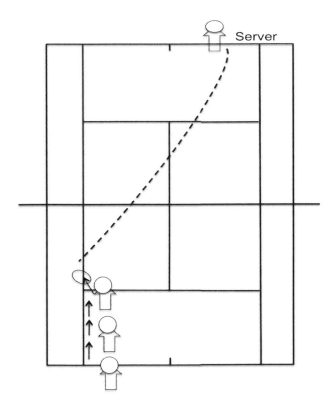

The returner should move
forward to cut off the sharp
angle from the spin serve.

Incorrectly Cutting Off The Angle

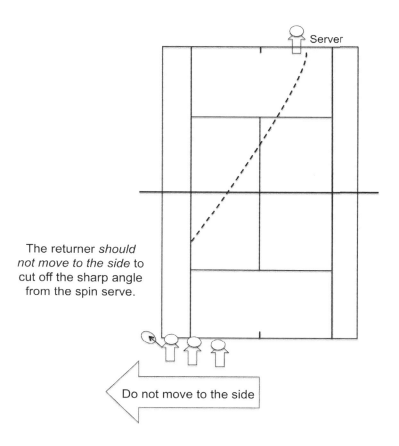

Server

The returner *should not move to the side* to cut off the sharp angle from the spin serve.

Do not move to the side

2. The Server's Toss

Prior to acknowledging an opponent's toss, returners must be aware of their own movement. Moving backwards to return the serve despite its speed and power is unnecessary. The returner should prepare with subtle motion to pounce on the serve. Since serves suddenly bound toward the returner, the briefest footwork is needed. The return-of-serve is akin to a spirited reach, a few fast footsteps and lots of anticipation.

The player who returns the serve should inquire: 1) Does the server place the toss routinely in the same spot? 2) Do links exist between those diversified tosses and where serves land in the court? Many players believe that scrutinizing these aspects requires them to do too much work. Yet prior to striking the ball, the returner merely watches and waits for the ball to leave the opponent's side to cross the net. Players will be surprised to learn the capabilities that they possess, to retain this tennis information if they only endeavor to experiment.

3. Momentum

One tactic has the returner position a few feet further back and then move forward at that precise second when the serve is struck. This forward movement propels returners' momentum and readiness. The motion sharpens vision, thrusting a returner to attack the oncoming serve, opposed to a returner who passively receives the serve and allows it to dominate. A player should attack the service by charging forth with momentum directly toward the ball. This aggressive return-of-serve skill is very effective in dulling the serve's force.

4. Stand Strong

The function of the torso requires great attention. Keep the torso upright and the chest open when approaching the serve. Instead of bending while waiting to return the serve, focus on the extended posture and the torso's upward lift. If the torso is bent over a second too long, the body is unable to straighten up in time to dart toward the ball. With the torso bent and the head set at a lower plane, vision will be joggled when rising suddenly upwards to track the serve. Swaying the head to and fro defies a player's precision and balance. Most tennis players should resist this head swaying as a general rule.

5. Skillful Hands and Feet

The return-of-serve exemplifies quick hands and feet. Players should keep their hands naturally relaxed in front of their torso. Returning serve is kindred to feeling the ball is struck with the palm. An excellent return-of-serve depends on players knowing *precisely* where their hands are. A sturdy torso structures the body, allowing more hand freedom to better manage the skill. The hands and feet team together in a synchronized effort to move forward and attack the approaching ball. The favorable phrase, "hands and feet," is a valuable reminder for a player to silently recap when returning serve.

6. Steer Clear of Making the Court Smaller for Your Opponent

The returner should be adamant not to return serves in the net. A return-of-serve struck into the net is a gift; the opponent(s) is unchallenged and does not even need to forge an attempt! If a player hauls the ball out or even wide, this manner of error is always preferable to sending the return into the net.

Players may inquire into the other reasons which prove striking the return-of-serve in the net is *so detrimental*. A ball scurrying into the net is relatively equivalent to a ball that barely jets over the net. If that same ball, per chance, crosses the net by a sheer 2 inches, this screeching return lands shorter in the court than had it carried more height. Its power will temper after it crosses the net. Therefore, your opponent, the server who already begins the point at an advantage only needs to apply a less than ordinary effort to block your oncoming power while remaining physically balanced and composed.

Players allot an undersized court for their opponents to play in when their return-of-serves skim the net by 2, 3, 6... inches, even by 1 foot. When the court is smaller, returners neglect to pressurize their opponents to any extreme or challenge their opponents to compete in the full-sized (78' x 36' or 78' x 27') court. Doubles players should be indifferent about how their opponents are positioning at the net and instead, concentrate solely on producing the best return-of-serves. The ball should be aimed for depth, to buy time and to craft a larger playing field which presents serving opponents with various obstacles when encountering the return.

7. Agility and Aggression

The return-of-serve combines agility skills distinctive from the established groundstroke used during a rally. The ball zooms into the service box from high above with a sharp trajectory potentially kicking to a player's shoulder height, possibly above the returner's head. The trajectory alone makes the serve more challenging to return than rallying with a regular groundstroke.

Therefore, returners must display aggressive foot speed, sharp vision, hand skill, flexibility and energy in unison to pounce on the return-of-serve.

Court Measurements

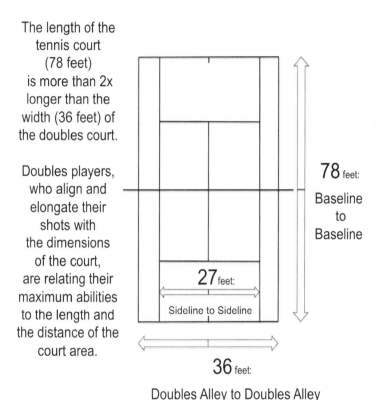

The length of the tennis court (78 feet) is more than 2x longer than the width (36 feet) of the doubles court.

Doubles players, who align and elongate their shots with the dimensions of the court, are relating their maximum abilities to the length and the distance of the court area.

78 feet:

Baseline to Baseline

27 feet:

Sideline to Sideline

36 feet:

Doubles Alley to Doubles Alley

8. Knowing What Makes You Fastest

Body types are seldom considered part of the strategy though each tennis player is equipped with unique movement. Physical movements that work for one player may hamper another. The counterparts of racquets, balls, court's dimensions and even tactics are constant yet player's body types are never uniform in shape. What matters are the individualistic features favoring each tennis player's tempo.

Each player must discover through self-experimentation how to best pounce on the returns. Remaining stationary and shifting weight on their toes benefits some returners. Other returners bend their knees low to the ground and spring upward for the pounce. Varieties for return-of-serve preparation exist and to assert that one athletic component is more worthwhile than another justifiably depends on the player's body type, strength and agility. Through trial and error, players become observant regarding their own athletic responses as they strike successful return-of-serves. This athletic introspection prompts returners to emulate their natural athletic abilities on a repetitive basis.

9. Smashing the Return-of-Serve

The trajectory of a level groundstroke, which rides parallel with the net, is different from a strong serve's trajectory that pops upward. A player receiving this serve's overleaping bounce has the option of using a smashing forehand or backhand return. Players should be alert to evade smashing the return-of-serve directly downward. This easy error is formed when striking the downward motion. Return-of-serves ought to sail over the net with a good margin of clearance. A smashing return, which cruises the net by 2, 3, 4, 5 and even 6 feet, ensures that the ball evades the net.

10. The Guessing Rule

This rule exhibits the last straw. Guessing is the best advice for those occasions when serves monopolize the score. This risky enterprise bodes well for players willing to gamble. Players must consider gambling on the return-of-serve when they find themselves completely unable to get their racquets on the ball. For instance, players may discover that only 1 of 4 serves is returned, hence another approach for returning serve must be applied. A returner needs to guess which lateral side the serve might bounce on and quickly sprint to the presupposed side at the precise moment when the serve is struck. If serves are too speedy and aimed into the body, the returner might consider backing up and running the body's movement and momentum toward the serve. This supportive motion also uses the serve's power to block the ball back into the court.

If, by happenchance a singles player or doubles team break (win) 1 of their opponent's dominating service games and win each of their own service games, the guessing players will have won the set. In doubles for instance, if both doubles players have trouble returning the opponent's serve, as a team they might make a pact to guess the serve's landing. When players break the server once per set, those doubles or singles players who unsuccessfully got their racquet on the majority of serves could actually end up winning the match. Just a few points can win a whole tennis match. Players should reflect on the strange phenomena that occur during competition.

Doubles players frequently believe their team movements such as charging the net are most essential. But more significantly, doubles players should communicate to each other when they error on return-of-serves, why they happened to error and how to change their return-of-serve results. Intelligent doubles is about understanding the nature of the errors as a team. The statistical outcomes of the serve and return-of-serve expose the most decisive influences on winning. Consequently, doubles players must vigorously communicate if they do not win their opponent's service games. If one doubles player alone happens to have great trouble returning serve and it looks like guessing is needed, a team conversation of encouragement favors the lone returner. In doubles, the return-of-serve is a joint effort. Doubles players should consider that the attention placed on running to the net and smashing balls might be better directed toward observing opponents' serves. In the situation of the left-handed server, for example, the lefty has potential to change the outcome of the entire match because the lefty creates an unwieldy spin for right-handers to return.

The profusion of artful singles and doubles tactics take a back seat to the importance of serves and return-of-serves, and the return-of-serve *must take precedence over other areas of the game*. It's at this juncture where players most often diverge their attention, abandoning their return-of-serve skill to focus heavily on the other areas of their games. Cutting-edge singles and doubles strategies can be pursued in shinning glory only after players develop a strong foundation regarding their serves and return-of-serves.

THE BASELINE T

One of a player's challenges is to produce a chockfull of winners on the sidelines, however the strongholds of a player's game first need to be cultivated. A player's delivery of direct, linear, laser-like shots is a stepping stone, an apprenticeship, for learning to precisely strike the sidelines. Although the space is elongated, the breadth of the tennis court is still more narrow than wide. Players who develop *feel* for the straight-lined shot progress to strike future sideline shots with ease.

The major distinction between recreational, tournament and league competitors compared to the touring tennis player is the respective usage of court space. This reflects a difference in players' intuitive understanding of the area. Once singles and doubles players are prepared with core attributes such as the awareness of extra court space and crisp serves and return-of-serves, these players should add a strategic durable tactic to their armory. This shot is created from forehands and backhand groundstrokes. A player should aim this shot to land on that center mark which shall be named the *Baseline T*. All players realize that this little, white mark insinuates the division of the court. Yet, do singles and doubles players recognize the value in attempting to strike this middle mark?

This effective shot will naturally guide players to develop a smooth, lined ball that travels deeply and extensively through the center of the court. Players may assume that this method is too simple, though it holds a world of tennis wisdom. Singles players commonly believe the only shots worthy of greatness are speedy shots that skid on the sidelines. An observation of flashiness and power emitted by tennis playing peers or touring competitors might tug at players' doubt. Despite the impressive strokes, players must question whether these sideline shots win tennis matches.

Contrary to general conjecture, players striking through the middle of the court utilize a covertly advantageous area. This shot leads players to interpret the Baseline T as a constant gauge of measure for the entire court. The Baseline T is similar to the function of a compass because it estimates the court from its center. In essence, the majority of strokes are actually straight-lined. Nonetheless, when players' aims are centered, not only do players have an easy constant guide as they play, their shots become shielded against inadvertent sideline errors.

How do players measure the area if they are unable to repeatedly find the court's perfect center and realms of depth? If the Baseline T shot is missed, players have merely erred with an offensive attempt. If the Baseline T shot is successful, the player has preferably landed the ball deep near the Baseline T. Practicing to strike the Baseline T increases players' stability, perception and measurement. This development leads players to eventually find the sidelines with great precision.

You should first approach the Baseline T at its idealistic advantages. Balls that land on the Baseline T mark challenge opponents to create angles. Your Baseline T shot uncomfortably nudges your opponents further behind the baseline than they would ever desire. Victorious winning shots are hard pressed to depart from opponent's racquets as they strain to swing 2 to 5 feet behind the baseline. Singles and doubles' opponents will both labor to swerve their shots to sharp angled aims from the brilliant balls you peg (or attempt to peg) on their Baseline T. Every ball bouncing off the tee mark roughly kicks up and back at least 2 to 5 feet. Baseline T shots acquire additional effects subject to artistic facets such as spins, power, height over the net, wind, etc...

Pace, Height, Depth

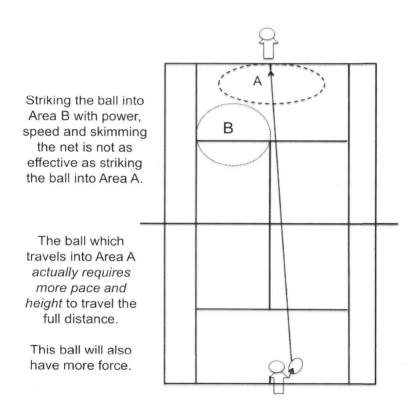

Striking the ball into Area B with power, speed and skimming the net is not as effective as striking the ball into Area A.

The ball which travels into Area A *actually requires more pace and height* to travel the full distance.

This ball will also have more force.

The idea of intentionally striking the Baseline T may appear plain and irrelevant as the significance of the Baseline T shot is illusory. Consider, if a player never wagers on the width of the sidelines and instead, judiciously aims down the court's center, vying for depth, distance and rhythm, this player has minimized uncalculated risk and accidental errors. So, players gain a valuable aptitude to work from the middle of the court - outward, reaping tremendous advantages. The Baseline T shot fine-tunes a player's timing, adjusts the tempo and places a player's game on track where play is free, agile and precise.

If you have trouble breaking service games and proceed to make it harder on yourself by creating a shot unfathomably out of sight, you've doubled your chances to lose the point. While receiving an opponent's potent swerving serve, your most enriching aim is to return through the center of the court. Recall, your return-of-serve is the "other first ball" you initiate into play and it accounts for your prime opportunity to make a statement for exactly half of the total games you will play! In singles, striking the ball through the middle has emerged as a notable contemporary plan for several reasons just mentioned. The most powerful skill a doubles player possesses is to be able to strike that center mark; the Baseline T.

What about the effectiveness in sending return-of-serves through the middle of the court especially when playing serve-and-volleyers? Serve-and-volley play is utterly beautiful with its consideration of opponents' weaker sides, instigated plans and appropriately executed serves. Sadly, serve-and-volley players are becoming extinct since they have more difficulty due to the technological power emanating from the racquets, strings and balls.

What if your singles opponent strikes with great power yet happens to slowly cover the court? Why would you want to strike through the middle toward the Baseline T? In doubles, what if opponents are positioned at the net, charging through the middle and poaching your returns into winners. Should you really abandon sending shots through the middle of the court to deter your opponents from poaching? The following section on scenarios and tactics discusses a player's questions regarding this contemporary shot. How players weigh the advantages versus disadvantages via each singles and doubles opponent encountered is one of the most important themes in tennis.

If you have nothing to lose, but instead you can instantly improve your tennis acumen, why wouldn't you transform and recreate your tennis game according to strategic analysis? You compete exactly as you interpret the game. Your tactics must be designed to be developmental and reflective of the results you wish to assemble in your match play. If you want instant improvement, use the court's center and send your shots to the Baseline T.

Let's now recognize how players can beneficially apply the down-the-middle concept, transforming singles and doubles strategies respectively.

SCENARIOS AND TACTICS FOR SINGLES

The concept of the Baseline T invokes inquiry whether sending the ball down the center of the court is useful against a slow moving opponent. Before players become concerned with their opponents, they really should concentrate on their own productivity and their strategic strength. Building a solid tennis structure is the most important aspect for a singles player. The intelligent player uses power down-the-middle to sustain safety and acquire rhythm simultaneously.

Pounding away down-the-middle pushes your opponents further back into the court. This tactic makes it difficult for them to create offensive shots. It matters little if your opponents are slow if you happen to error with your sideline shots. The main idea is to create a safe place to strike the ball with your power. Your opponents may become complacent with your manner of play which could slacken their judgment. Your opponents could easily relax, assuming that all your balls will filter through the middle of the court. Meanwhile, you are warming up to gain rhythm, to surprise your opponent with your mixture of sharp angles. This platform of command is simplified, deceptive and strong. Your opponents have no way to read your mind and they become susceptive to your consistency and cadence.

Once players have fundamentally developed their base strengths, they can effectively apply their other creative shots. Without this reliable foundation, creative shots will lose their brilliance. 1 great creative shot amidst 4 creative errors such as sideline mistakes, net mistakes, return-of-serve errors or a ball landing too short goes unnoticed in the score. Players tend to remember their remarkable shots but forget to regard how they lose points. Striking the ball deeply and powerfully through the middle of the court creates a sturdy tennis architecture any player can adapt to. The down-the-middle ploy is also secure for the return-of-serve. The additional advantages of striking powerfully through the middle are that shots will stay inside the court on windy days. A player develops a sense of working from inside the court – outward. The singles court is spacious because it has significant length (78 feet long) but it has only 27 feet of width. The further away the target is, the skinnier the width becomes lending it to be more difficult to place the ball within the confines of its narrowness. Give or take a few feet, the singles court's length is almost 3x its width! Considering the trajectory of the ball gains distance with elevation (soaring over the net), the ball travels even further than 78 feet from one baseline to the other. Deploying these down-the-middle tactics insures that players' foundational strengths are built up for their eventual creative play.

As a singles player, you come to the match equipped with this simplified plan. With intention to strike through the middle, you are ready to comfortably test your opponents in a number of ways. At the start of the match, determine where your opponent strikes their first 4 or 5 shots from your deep middle shot. Keep the results in your memory. Many players believe keeping track of their opponent's abilities and tactics is too much work. If you have a contained focus regarding your own game, you are able to use the extra energy to store the information about your opponent in your tennis memory bank.

When aiming deeply through the court's center, ask these questions about your opponent:

Singles Players' Inquiry

- Where do my opponent's balls land?

- Do my opponent's shots travel short?

- Do my opponent's shots travel in angles to my forehand or backhand side?

- Do my opponent's shots travel low?

- Do my opponent's shots travel high?

- Do my opponent's shots travel with topspin?

- Do my opponent's shots travel with backspin?

Gather this information on what your opponent creates in the first few games. You gain a good sense regarding the higher probability of their shot choices. Opponents are liable to change tactics throughout time though most players perform in the beginning of their matches analogous to their naturalistic styles.

For instance, if your opponents strike balls low, lift your shots higher over the net for more depth. Sending shots down-the-middle and deep should be your starting focal point. To emulate your opponents' shots is not the best plan. Your opponents may be setting you up for the types of shots they would prefer to receive. This deems why you must have your own independent approach equipped with a mental inventory assessment.

A first-ball strike in a singles match is the very first ball that the server will strike *after serving*. Players must recall that their main focus is to win their service games. As a player, you have command and time to decide each serve and do you really want to risk an error with the first chance you get from your opponent's return-of-serve? This seemingly insignificant question calls for much introspection. Your service games are assured to win more than your return-of-serve games unless you develop a return-of-serve that matches the command of your serve. If you must absolutely pummel the ball, think about aiming toward the center with a tad of racquet-face angle. This insures that the ball keeps within the sidelines and simultaneously heads in the lateral direction. At the same time, the ball will carry loads of power as the shot is safely aimed near the middle of the court. This option is a player's choice. Aiming for the sideline with all of your power may result in 1 or 2 winners per service game, but if 3 attempted winners are missed within the same service game, the play is ineffective.

The first-ball strike suggests that a player has an affinity with a favorite shot. Maybe the particular type of shot used on first-ball strike is the strongest shot a player has. In that case, a player should use their preferred winning shot. The options depend on the player's skill. Consequently, the preference to use the first-ball strike varies because players must count the number of winners and winning points versus the losing points they have acquired per game to make appropriate choices on whether to use their first-ball strike.

As a match proceeds and your concentration intensifies, you may want to send 2 powerful down-the-middle shots and then creatively produce a drop shot. An opponent needs to run a long distance, 30-40 feet from behind the baseline to the net. Today's speed and power have replaced sideline shots as being a player's only advantages. So, if you love to volley, you need not wait for the moment to strike the sidelines to come in. Instead, strike powerfully deep to the Baseline T mark and rush to the net. Your opponent will be hard-pressed to create sharp angles and you could prosper with a sharp volley. The point will be shortened so make sure that you put the volley away. The results could tally toward further success or reduce the positive outcome.

Although your aspiration will be to produce a creative array of strikes, you must play resolutely with your serve and return-of-serve strongholds. As points ensue, striking balls through the middle will be extremely effective. You will be able to analyze your opponents and adjust your game quickly to the match pressures. As a bonus, by issuing balls through the middle, you familiarize yourself with how to continually restore your game to its original and dependable state. Players must know that adding creativity always alters the winning statistic. Making sure you have a firm base of consistency to spring your future creative shots such as your sideline shots, spins and power is wise.

SCENARIOS AND TACTICS FOR DOUBLES

PART 1: THE PLAN

Doubles Scenario

It's the beginning of the match.

You and your doubles partner face a doubles team; one player serves and the other player is at the net.

Plan

Test each of your opponents early in the match with your returns-of-serves.

Strike 16 experimental shots to test each of your opponents.

4 down-the-middle
4 lobs
4 angled cross-courts
4 alley shots

Testing your opponents with 4 select shots of any type is a good number. 2 winning volleys struck by an opponent could have been accidental, 3 winning volleys struck by an opponent hints that the poacher is comfortable at the net, but 4 winner volleys confirm an opponent's strength. If the net opponents easily put away volleys from a low middle shot, do they have difficulty with a higher ball travelling through the middle of the court?

Early, halfway through the 1st set, you need and want a planned offensive play toward your opponents. Your team will learn exactly what your opponents are capable of, and where their weaknesses lie. Doubles teams are frequently in doubt regarding their opponents' true strengths and weaknesses even when regularly playing the same opponents. At times, players might become impressed or shocked with opponents' winners, viewing them as masterpieces. The irony is that those great winners could have been accidental! Players need to test their opponents to gain a refined assessment of what truly transpires during a match.

An inquiry presented on the following page provides you with questions to obtain knowledge on each of your opponents. Keep your opponents' tennis stats recorded in your tennis memory. While you compete, take a stockpile of mental notes. Examine your opponents' preferences during the earliest stages of a match. Since opponents are liable to change their tactics, being alert to what opponents deliver in the match moment to moment disbands the surprises created from their agendas.

The following *Doubles Players' Inquiry* contains questions which doubles players should ask themselves during those moments in-between points and games.

Doubles Players' Inquiry

- Where do my opponents' serves land most of the time?

- Do my net opponents poach "winning volleys" from both my backhand and forehand returns?

- Do my net opponents cross through the middle every time I strike the ball?

- Do my net opponents make outright volley winners or basically put the ball back into play?

- Do my net opponents move to the ball only when it appears closer to where they stand?

- Are my net opponents successful or unsuccessful, 4 points out of 4 from my middle shot? My lobs, angled crosscourt, and alley shots?

Is asking this stock of questions too taxing for a player during competition? Well, without a strong strategic framework, players' random choices will leave their efforts meandering and unreliable. Improvement really depends on understanding what occurs on the court according to what your opponents present. General opinion trusts that improvement will happen by playing often. This common attitude, which does not inquire into the character of the game, is void of court cleverness. Therefore, bring your inquiry to the court, observe it in action, experience the results. Exercising these questions to yourselves on the court will quickly become second nature. As a partnership, your doubles team will be equipped with the criterion to analyze your competitors.

Scenarios and Tactics For Doubles

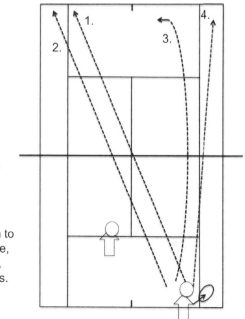

Plan

1. Middle
2. Angled Cross Courts
3. Lobs
4. Alley Shots

The returner should plan to strike 4 down-the-middle, 4 angled cross-courts, 4 lobs, and 4 alley shots.

What if you realize that your net opponents decline to take full advantage of your middle returns? You continue to strike with the most effective shot. If your opponents strike 4 for 4 winning volleys from your middle returns, you gain 1 important statistical fact in the very beginning of the match. You will stop losing points throughout the remainder of play because you are aware to evade sending shots through the middle with this doubles opponent. This collected knowledge is valuable for your inventory on your opponents. Both scenarios present good news for you, giving you key information which you would lack without the tester.

If you recognize that your opponents successfully make 4 of 4 volley winners from your mid-court ball, you immediately refocus, changing your mix of returns. Test your net opponents with the other shots: 4 lobs, 4 alley shots and 4 angled cross-courts. And never let the poacher intimidate you because the player parades around the net like a lion.

Your mentally documented facts reveal the advantages of structured strategic knowledge. You must notice that your player inquiry creates multiple advantages and insight which overwhelmingly outweighs the disadvantage of losing a few points. Without the follow-up inquiry, a player lacks an edged artifice. Players must ask themselves questions to profit from their opponents positive and negative capabilities.

Being aware of the area where the server delivers the serve to you is very important. If your opponent uses both the forehand and the backhand sides of the service box, you will instantly recognize the synchronization regarding your return-of-serves. Identifying your opponents' strengths especially in these beginning stages of the match is your great advantage. You have control in regards to your plan and your intention. Instead of trying to read your mind or configure your plan, your opponents are mostly likely too concerned with what they are attempting to do.

The inquiry is also used for analyzing opponents during the midst of a match. Final results of every point can almost be backtracked to what occurred with the serve and the return-of-serve. Servers have options to change types of serves used. A server can stand in different places to create sharper angles, throw more spin onto the serve or focus on opponent's weaker return sides. If your team is losing and you both are positioned at the net, stay back, retreat to the baseline more. Experiment and observe what occurs. Do your planned changes jumble the poacher's results? Have a cache of questions and choices ready at hand.

Reconsider the court's dimensions. Players must be familiar with the significance of the middle of the court. The mid line is equally distant from the alley sideline. If the returner misses by 1 inch when striking through the middle or the alley line, the point is lost. If a returner misses by 2-10 inches when striking through the court's middle, the team stays in the point. In doubles, striking the ball through the center has equivalent value to striking the ball precisely onto the alley line. Plus, your net opponent presumably covers at least one-half of the court, positioning near the center of that space. A ball landing on the alley line requires the net opponent to reach approximately the same distance as a ball that would land in the center.

Nearly Equidistant

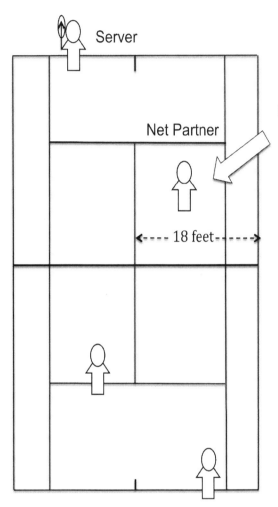

Server

Net Partner

←---- 18 feet ---→

Even though the net partner is nearer to the mid line than to the alley, in reality this player is still positioned almost equally distant from the center to the alley line, give or take a foot of distance.

PART 2

SCENARIOS AND TACTICS FOR DOUBLES
THE DOUBLES ALLEY AND CHARGING THE NET

Use the alleys
more often in
doubles.

Returns struck
into the alleys
open up the
court.

Let your doubles
partner know
when you plan on
returning into the
alley.

This way your net
partner can *be
ready* to attack
the volley return.

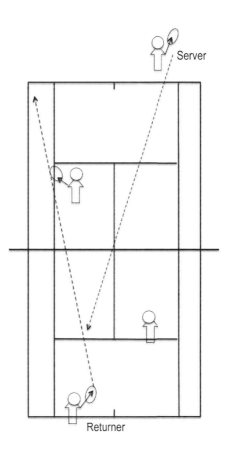

Server

Returner

Doubles Scenario

You are returning a serve.
Your doubles partner is ready at the service line.

Your doubles opponents could either be:
1) one player at the baseline and the other at the net
or
2) both doubles opponents at the net

Tactic

You send your return-of-serve down the alley.

Should you follow your shot by charging the net?

- Does your team specifically understand the reasons why charging the net are meant to be effective?

- Why is it wise to frequently use the alleys?

- What should your doubles team expect from your intended alley shot?

Let's first discuss the alley return. Many players discount using the alley because they assume that their opponents will cover those shots. Consequently, these players perceive that the entire court is covered. Players must not assume that their opponents are capable of hitting every ball back until proven! Many doubles players disregard the alley because it's unknown territory. On rare occasion, doubles players may strike in that area yet they are unaccustomed to hitting in that portion of the court. Other players are unfamiliar with designs ensuing when they actually do strike the alley since they attempt it sparingly. Some doubles players are so intent on charging the net that their focus is controlled by their forward movement instead of on a particular purpose or plan other than getting to the net.

The alley shot is effective for various reasons. When you strike into the alley, you keep both of your opponents honest and constantly guessing. *Your shots* become unpredictable for your opponents. The alley shot opens up the court by pulling net opponents slightly off to the side. Just because opponents are positioned at the net does not imply that their volleys will be successful. Sadly, doubles players often focus specifically to hit the ball further away from opponents. Consequently, these doubles players are prone to miss due to the additional demand they apply to their own shots. With slight illogicality, opponents sometimes return shots better when they have to struggle and stretch, rather than to balls struck nearby or directly hit where they are positioned.

Doubles players need to be well informed about why charging the net is deemed an effective plan. Although doubles players should advance toward the net, the solid reasons why players habitually charge the net are few. A doubles team who gets a hold of the ball first while stationed at the net has the opportunity to promptly win the point. *But*, if the doubles team does not win the point from their 1st volley, let's hope the volley was a powerful shot otherwise this doubles team literally hands the reign to their opponents. This place is exactly the situation where players want to avoid getting caught; they secure the advantage but then easily hand it back to opponents because their 1st volley was either too mild, or too fast and short.

What generates the success or the demise of a volley is not necessarily the volley itself. Players often miss a volley and believe it's strictly a physical, technical error when the error is really comprised of intricacy. The error typically recurs without players ever knowing why. The faster the volley is sent over the net, the quicker it "boomerangs" into your court. So exactly *why* are doubles players customarily instructed to rush the net? The real substance ought to be in teaching players to develop a good sense of what their opponents are capable of, that mental inventory regarding opponents' probabilities and then proceed from there.

The purpose of rushing the net in doubles is ensconced in the idea that the first player to get the racquet on the volley finishes the point. If winning points do not occur on a consistent basis, doubles players should reassess how often they want to rush the net. The other main purpose in rushing to the net in doubles is to cut off the angle from the opponent's shots. Both situations require players have an intuitive assessment of their opponents' abilities. Naively charging toward the net without this awareness is to compete unproductively.

When doubles players rush the net, they better put the ball away from the beginning otherwise the ball may rebound into their court giving them scant time to react. Many doubles players believe that running up to the net during every point is the proper approach for their doubles play. But teams must ask themselves if this ploy is truly effective for winning matches? When players play too close to the net, they have almost no time to respond. Hopefully, their 1st volley shot was an outright winner or returned weakly otherwise these players have issued a most unfavorable tactic. Volleying at the net suitably depends on players' retrieval skills, quickly wrenching themselves to the back portion of the service box to gain time.

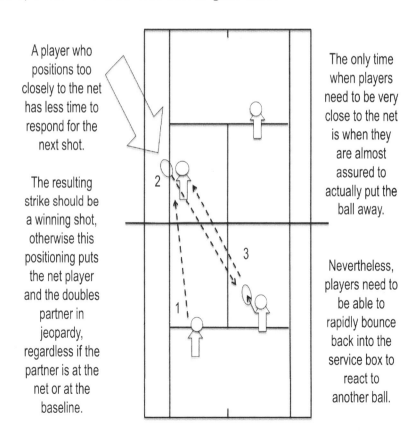

A player who positions too closely to the net has less time to respond for the next shot.

The resulting strike should be a winning shot, otherwise this positioning puts the net player and the doubles partner in jeopardy, regardless if the partner is at the net or at the baseline.

The only time when players need to be very close to the net is when they are almost assured to actually put the ball away.

Nevertheless, players need to be able to rapidly bounce back into the service box to react to another ball.

Cutting off the angle explains why players go to the net since the further the ball sails out of the doubles court, the more difficult the shot is to control. A player's intent should be to strike the ball before it exits with an angle out of the court. Conversely, when you are the player who strikes the alley, you are creating a certain angle. Drawing opponents off the court, you have opportune moments to hit the ball into the open area.

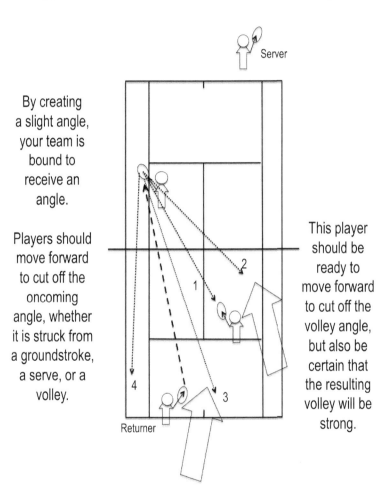

Server

By creating a slight angle, your team is bound to receive an angle.

Players should move forward to cut off the oncoming angle, whether it is struck from a groundstroke, a serve, or a volley.

This player should be ready to move forward to cut off the volley angle, but also be certain that the resulting volley will be strong.

Returner

The idea of cutting off the angle has not changed but the tennis evolution has transformed the game of doubles. Today, baseliners can also be extremely effective as doubles players, setting up the court for the net partner. Baseliners can work the entire court for their doubles' partners. The technological power of the racquets has enhanced this aspect.

Some players charge the net in doubles because they feel that it's fun. But the question again asks whether this tactic reliably wins matches? Inquiring how deeply a doubles team wants to win is a sharper approach. Players must be frank and scrutinize whether charging the net is the appropriate play for each individual point. Since balls arrive 2 to 3 times faster to the net player compared to the ball's arrival for the baseliner, *doubles players need to be 2 to 3 times quicker to react with their physical movements.*

Taking inventory on doubles opponents, you acquire an enhanced impression on what you should expect. This opposes tactics where players are geared to charge the net to which they encounter unsuspecting surprises every time they arrive. You must play the ball, play the dimensions of the court, pay attention to serves, return-of-serves and use your strategic inquiry and creative designs.

TENNIS STATS

The charted statistics of a tennis match present specific sections where players should focus to produce the best result. Tactics without strategic backup are simply artistic maneuvers lacking a plan on how to win. Up to this point, the importance of serves and return-of-serves has been established. As you interpret the elements listed in the general stats and facts chart, precedence is generally given in the following order: aces (the dominance of the serve), double faults (the weakness of the serve), 1st serves points won, 2nd serves points won, return-of-serve points won and break points won (points won from the return-of-serve games). The remaining percentages come from winners, unforced errors and net approaches.

Singles and doubles players should pay swift attention to the stats chart. The items listed in the stats chart rule. A singles player is decidedly aware that a good or poor result is mostly an individual matter. A singles player is relegated to cover the entire singles court and realizes that broad approaches must be followed. Doubles players often perceive that their dynamics should be exceedingly different from singles players, but the important aspects of both forms are congruent. At intensified levels regarding tour players, singles and doubles tactics do fluctuate with difference. At the same time, singles players possess stalwart features equally applicable for doubles players. Have you noticed that the same statistical chart is utilized for both singles and doubles? This reasoning illustrates precisely why singles and doubles features are comparable.

Concentration on strengthening areas in the stats chart is more relevant than employing secondary tactics. Sometimes doubles players' games are strong yet they believe they do not win because they lack knowledge on "how to play as a team." 20 years ago that theme would have been true though because of the present technological élan and players' athleticism, this ideology of knowing *how to play as a team* now ebbs and flows. The serves and the return-of-serves have been intensified as outstanding strategic components.

Singles players accept 100% of their results. Although with a loss, singles players should always give credit to winning opponents. Each doubles player accepts 100% of responsibility, which creates a combined 200% effort. This signifies that each doubles player must maximize winning percentages, avoiding a curt strategy which wins one partner 9 points but eventually contributes to losing the whole match. Doubles players believe that their plans of staying physically close on the court such as, "tied together with a string" and "charging the net," reveal the premise of playing doubles. This method is only effective when the primary constitution of the sport is strong which is what this book is all about.

The stats have the final say, presenting the significant elements of match play. Let's continue this journey towards the eye-opening experience that tennis statistics bring to light.

Tennis Stats

Aces
Double Faults
1st Serves
2nd Serves
Receiving Points Won (Return-of-Serves)
Break Points Won (from Return-of-Serves)
Winners
Unforced Errors
Net Approaches
Total Points Won

An Aerial View

Peering out from an airplane window seat, have you ever noticed a tennis court stretched out on the earth's terrain? Were you impressed at how elongated those faraway courts appeared from the clouds? You probably didn't give much thought to the court dimensions. However, those stretched out, narrow tennis courts mirror the same literal dimensions as the court which you compete on.

The view could also have the opposite effect. Capturing an image from such a distance could lead a player to believe that the court is quite small. Nevertheless, tactics for singles and doubles play must regard the court's linear measurements and scope. Tennis players should transform their strategies to align with the court's regional breadth. This contrasts methods where players skillfully learn tactics but refute the fundamental importance of the court's dimensions. Players equipped with this court dimensional expertise will highly contrast players who have never been led to recognize the court's extremity.

The latest racquet technologies have exceedingly aided in supplementing additional power for all players. Despite the innovation, the tennis court undergoes a feeble interpretation with the untrained eye. Familiar instructional tennis tends to focus on specified strategies like striking the ball away from an opponent or fashioning a complex choice of shots during the point. Nonetheless, without a conspicuous study of the tennis court itself and a player's keen relationship to its dimensions, the strategic designs can baffle players. This confusion is a result of former instructional technique continually influencing contemporary play.

Power has revolutionized tennis, hence the analysis of the sport should be revised at the same rapid rate. Accordingly, the concept of *feel* should be reintroduced to correspond with both the power and the court. *Feel* reflects a player's control and it contends why the court must be viewed differently than ever before. Future players should consider experimenting in the outer court boundaries to ripen their tennis ability and their sense of *feel* to the maximum degree.

An Element of *Feel*

The Skill of the Racquet-Head Tilt

The purpose of this demonstration is to show that a ball departing from the court's center requires only a tad of angle to go to either sideline.

The ball travels into the far corners of the court with only a slight adjustment, a subtle angle in the racquet-head.

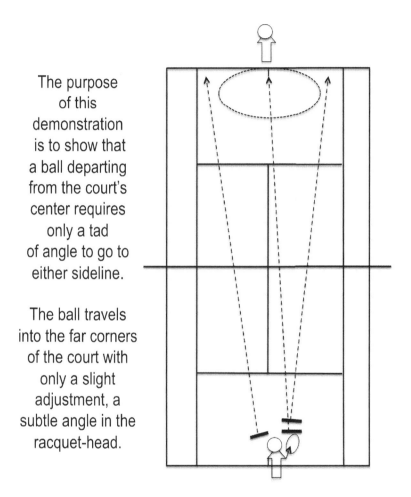

3 STAGES AFTER THE BOUNCE

Tennis offers myriads of surprise with each bounce that a ball takes. Throughout the course of a match, players may encounter various speeds, slants, kicks, skids, spins and angles as they calculate the site of the bounce for their strikes of *feel*. As a result from the bounce, intricate challenges exist other than hurriedly arriving to the ball. Players must judge the nature of the ball, its travel, its trajectory and its destination. Different types of courts affect the roles of the ball's bounce. Court surfaces tend to favor particular bounces hence they are supportive of players' individualistic styles. Perhaps one of the intriguing marvels about tennis happens when a player receives the character of the ball's bounce.

A good quality place to strike the ball is when it sits at its peak. When the ball is met at its peak, the ball has bounced, ascended, then holds for a split second in mid air before it begins to dip again. Players need to position themselves with comfortable proximity and in good balance to strike the ball at its peak. The advantages are inherent because the ball is still laden with force from the ground. Since the ball has not begun to dip, the ball is lighter for players to strike as compared to when the ball begins to drop. Fittingly, a player uses the power from the spring of the ball. Opponents also have less time to recapture their balance when receiving balls from players who hit the ball's peak.

The Peak

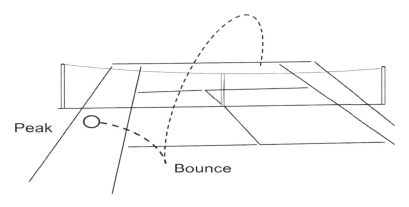

This ball has bounced and rises to its max.
The player who strikes this ball hits the ball at it's peak.

After the ball bounces and peaks, it descends for its second bounce and drops. A player who strikes the ball at this juncture is hitting the ball "late." Although this method is not incorrect, this delay is the least favorite for a few reasons. The opponent has a little more time to recover from the last shot. As the ball drops, it is a bit heavier and more difficult to control, as opposed to a ball sitting lightly at its peak. The only benefit that a player has while a ball drops is gaining a bit of extra time before actually hitting the ball. Extra time never hurts but this gives extra time to opponents who are also waiting for the shot to cross the net.

Letting the Ball Drop

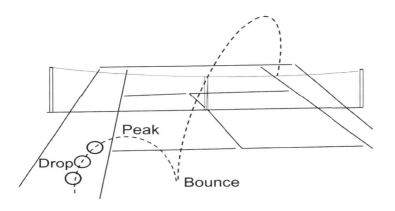

Anywhere on this range, where these 3 balls are viewed,
demonstrates letting the ball drop, or striking the ball
late.

The most advanced method of striking the ball is when
the ball rises. This occurs before the ball ascends to its peak.
Players must have great timing to strike balls as they leap off
the ground because the assorted bounces vary in pace and
direction. An opponent's shots must be well-read so the player
knows exactly what types of balls to expect. The advantage of
striking the ball on the rise is that it takes time away from
opponents that they would have had otherwise, if the player
had let the ball continue to ascend to its peak. Striking the ball
on the rise is furthermore effective because the power ejects
with immediacy due to its closeness to the court. The racquet-
head impact combined with the hasty spring of the bounce
creates added power. Thus, when the ball travels back to the
other side of the net, it departs speedily. A player's feet must
quickly position near the bounce since the ball is struck sooner

and requires more precision. The sharpest way for players to strike the ball is on the rise which might be anywhere on that ascension path. If players can successfully strike the ball on the rise, it can be a powerful tool.

On the Rise

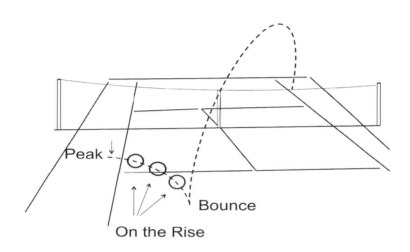

On the Rise

THE COURT WITHIN A COURT

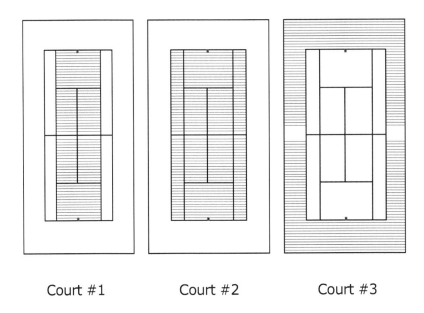

Court #1   Court #2   Court #3

This illustration shows a singles court (Court #1) and a doubles court (Court #2) interposed within the outer frame of the tennis court (Court #3). These courts, inside and outside, should be regarded and experienced to their fullest degree. This opposes the belief that the only space worthy of tennis players' attention is the court that contains the service lines, sidelines and baselines.

These 3 courts target distinctive ways to conceptualize the court region. The marked extra lines demonstrate that both the singles and doubles courts are subconsciously measured by invisible increments of space. Hence, the courts' conventional lines (the baseline, sidelines, service line...) combined with the invisible, incremental spatial measurements (those added lines seen on Courts #1, #2 and #3) must be acknowledged and scrutinized to a very fine extent.

Stated differently, players do not predict measurements by gazing at the lines of a geometric court. The way in which players measure the area and distances inside the court is by contrasting space with the outer regions of the court. When players step onto the court, they generally perceive the court as a vast space with a few white lines, contrary to how people accurately measure distance. The purpose and rationale behind this discussion is to dissect the court into fragments. A player should stringently measure the area around the baseline and sidelines. Instead of noticing vast court space, the room near the lines ("in" and "out") must be assessed. Players tend to only want to know the inside of the court. Nevertheless, being equally cognizant to the outer region promotes a refined and more perfected measurement of the tennis court. Striking the ball "out" of the court is an action that measures where the tennis court actually resides.

This exercise emphasizes the attainment of command rather than holding back with resistance and fear of hitting out. Since racquets project power to perform mesmerizing results, players must be encouraged not only to experiment inside the court but also outside of the court field as well. This spatial modernization leads players to improve *feel*. *Feel* originates from an agile hand. Angles maneuvered by the palm's slant simultaneously reflect the racquet handle and the racquet-face.

By calculating all spatial measurements with *feel*, players sensing their ball placement on the other side of the court with the palm of their hand develop an acute faculty when striking groundstrokes. This notion regarding *feel* is very different from guessing, that looser estimation which players use to land the ball in the general vicinity of their desire.

Every singles and doubles player should acknowledge the importance of *feel* above technique. *Feel* is the fundamental mark that impacts tennis performance. If a player truly wants to advance, a strong focus on the nature of the hand suffices.

Focus key attention on the connection between your hand, your mental concentration and the areas within the court to cultivate *feel*.

An Element of *Feel*

The Skill of the Racquet-Head Tilt

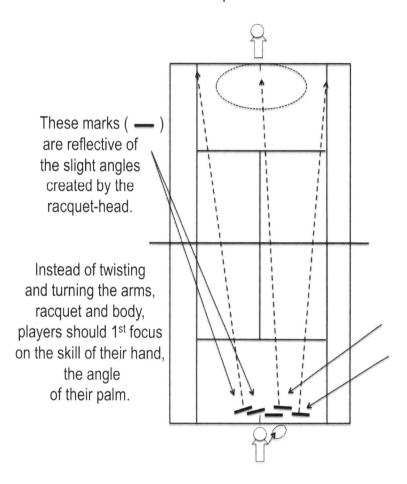

These marks (—)
are reflective of
the slight angles
created by the
racquet-head.

Instead of twisting
and turning the arms,
racquet and body,
players should 1st focus
on the skill of their hand,
the angle
of their palm.

THE RELEVANCE OF EXTRA SPACE

To dramatically progress, players must at times step out of their comfortable zones, staying open to innovative activity. The most fitting time for players to discover their own potential is to experiment with a particular technique or drill. This curious reflection is meant to enhance a player's comprehension, court-sense, *feel* and potential amassed in the extraordinary skills of measurement.

Most tennis players tend to roll their eyes and shut their ears at a request to purposely hit the ball out. Yet, discovering the space situated on the other side of the court behind the baseline is imperative for every singles and doubles players' development. To speed up and sharpen measurement, a player should launch the ball beyond the boundaries of the lines. This evocative skill has players contrast the court's inner region to its outer region. Launching the ball frees up a player's swing, polishes a player's perception and pinpoints precisely where the baseline is located on the other side of the net. This technique could lead you to the most significant breakthrough you will ever have in fine-tuning your sense of court measurement.

Why do you need an aptitude for that area designated as "out"? Every player needs to acquire a precise feel for this region. A white painted line on a tennis court never determines a player's comprehensive ability to measure the entire space. The space around a baseline, or sideline, or service line includes both the area behind the line (out) and the area in front of the line (inside). This subconscious method that contrasts these relationships between inside and outside the court is one major way which players measure their singles and doubles court.

This method exposes the player's instinctive impression of the regional space located behind the baseline. Many players misleadingly believe that they are adept at striking balls out. Nonetheless, players should take an inventory to establish how truly consistent their aims are *outside of the court*. From the results, they discover that striking the ball a couple of feet out consistently and in the same region is difficult. In fact, the *feel* to strike the ball a few feet out is virtually identical to striking the ball a few feet inside the court.

A player should experiment by striking forehands and backhands to land balls 1 foot out, then 2 feet out, then 3 feet out, then 4 feet out, et cetera. Not surprisingly, players clutch a whopping resistance to accept any technique that does not promise instant success or appears to oppose general belief. Players hesitate to accept purposely hitting out *until they notice rapid improvement* in measuring space closer to the baseline. This discovery is a process in truly learning the court's breadth.

You, the reader, may want take one moment to reason the sports logic: If a player precisely launches a ball with ease, 90 and 100 feet away with each single strike, then toning down the strike and bringing the ball "in," aiming only 80 feet (as opposed to 90 or 100 feet) is a piece of cake! Tennis players rarely view their abilities or the court in this manner. Players commonly rebuff this mode of practice for they have fear of sailing the ball outside the court lines when actual competition ensues. Yet, striking the ball into the net is futile. If a ball sails into the net, even if the ball crosses the net by a few inches, the glide is so low that the shot will not make it to the court's depths. Striking the ball "out" broadens a player's aptitude for measurement with strength combined. Resistance by avoiding the outer zones sadly stunts players' tennis growth. Ironically, when players sail a ball out by 3 feet, they cringe as if they have made the worst mistake in the universe. An attempt to use the full tennis court should be a major theme when aiming.

How should players ever really know where the baseline is if they lack true perception where a few feet beyond the baseline is? How do players develop true perfect precision if they are apprehensive to strike a ball a little bit out? This skill depicts one's tennis acumen combined with physical strength. A player's ability is rooted in this combination of tennis strength and sensory capacities of measurement. The premise is about precision, strength and *feel*.

The idea is to develop the proclivity to access the entire tennis court with ease. The key is that if a player has never consistently struck ball after ball with precise intent to land a ball exactly 7 feet, or exactly 3 feet or exactly 4 feet outside the baseline, then this player's faculty to measure area 80-90 feet from one baseline to the other is transparently foreign. This skill becomes more apparent when players find themselves "on the run." Without this experience, a player possesses a vague sense of measurement since the flight of the ball in that space is unchartered territory. A professional tennis player has spent years and thousands and thousands of hours aiming at the baseline. The outer parts of the court have been accessed more abundantly than the recreational tennis players who play for enjoyment. Whether or not it was intentionally initiated, the exorbitant training naturally enhanced the tour player's ability to form acute perceptions of the whole court through the tides of measurement.

The drill is beneficial for 2 major reasons: this practice concurrently enhances court-sense and precisonal court aim. A player's ability to measure lengthy latitudes is commonly given unstipulated attention. Tennis players should not only learn the court from *inside to out*, they should also learn the court from *outside, back in*. This expansive exercise not only provokes the use of the court's entire scope through experimentation, it frees and opens up a groundstroke. This treasured approach reveals the court's "out" sections are subconsciously used to measure where each incremental section "inside" the court is located.

Do you know why players find it an easy task to aim a groundstroke inside, or near the service line? The reason is because players are accustomed to aim within the larger court. Players who develop strengthened perception feel the court has become smaller and closer in proximity. Instead of being frugal with their strengths, players ought to be extravagant with their tendencies to become much physically stronger than what is required. The tennis court concludes at the baseline but a player's expertise and strength shouldn't stop there too. The blend of precision with strength is what everyone should strive for.

This practice method is the fastest way to speedily upturn a player's aptitude. Generating this golden precision from outside to inside the court can also be applied to sidelines, serves, return-of-serves, volleys, overheads and all other shots.

Applying this process enables both singles and doubles players to assess every foot of measurement extending beyond the major lines. How could it be imagined that launching the ball beyond bounds immensely accelerates players' improvement? Experimentation leads players to speedily develop an expansive discernment for that immense space inside the large tennis court!

THE BLUEPRINT DRILL

This recommendation requests that you discover your spatial calculations of the tennis court by taking an inventory of your precision and consistency. The objective of *The Blueprint Drill* is to observe where your shots actually land. This drill is administered to you by another person with a basket of balls, as the emphasis is on utter placement and pure skill.

The drill requests that you aim 100 balls with precisional purpose to intentionally land each of your shots on the baseline itself. Ultimate concentration must be applied when you strike each individual ball, steadfastly aiming the ball to land precisely on the baseline. One major difference about this concentrated drill is that keen attention focuses on each individual ball, one ball at a time. Intense concentration should be amassed on each solitary surmounting shot. Every ball struck is treated as if it is the most crucial shot you will ever hit. You want each ball to literally land on the baseline.

Take your time, sojourn a moment between each of your strokes from one shot to the next. A shortened pause should ensue after each exclusive shot has landed on the other side of the court. Unlike other dashing aerobic tennis drills used for sprinting action and endurance, this drill is performed slowly in one stationary place. This meticulous drill is administered to find how precise you can be in the most stagnant condition.

What a player assembles on the run has roots in this deep-seated skill of precision.

After you have struck each individual ball, stop and have someone place a marker or an indicator to preserve the place where your ball landed. Use a blue or yellow cone or paper cup, making sure it doesn't fly away in the wind. Hit the shot, place the marker, then resume with your next shot.

After purposefully striking a total of 100 balls, you are ready to fully document your tennis skill inventory. Walk to the other side of the court where the markers have been placed and count the number of balls that landed near the baseline. Note the isolated balls that stopped short of the baseline. Note those particular balls that surpassed the baseline too.

With a rendition of a sketched tennis court, take precise notation by jotting down exactly where each ball landed. This drilling exercise perfectly demonstrates where your aims and your court perception are at the present moment. This exercise alludes to a journey toward your novel progress.

The Blueprint Drill reveals a tennis player's true ability to hit the baseline and the rest of the space inside the baseline. The purpose of this drill is to lead singles and doubles players to use the most distant area of the court. Without players' clear realization of their own abilities, recognizing where their shots consistently land is blurred. Hours of fortuitous practice can be good cardiovascular exercise yet practicing elusive aims ignores the precision and the perfection necessary to achieve constant advancement.

The authenticity of *The Blueprint Drill* marks a beginning in your transformation. It implores you to practice a method that ripens your court awareness. The data and percentages generated from your blueprint exemplify exactly what you will mathematically execute as you compete. The blueprint reveals how much court you really use on a regular basis when you attempt to aim deep into the court.

Singles and doubles players should apply this *Blueprint Drill* onto the all-encompassing scope of their serves, volleys, overheads, sidelines shots, return-of-serves and every possible shot that they create. As mentioned earlier, a salient difference between the touring player and recreational player is in their implicit awareness of the court's ample space. The tennis court space *perceived* by professionals is overwhelmingly large. Once players understand that this significant theme holds back their improvement, their development will momentously advance.

COURT-SENSE

Movement is one of the most complex subjects in tennis as it involves strength, agility, timing, flexibility, body type and other physical matters. Taking adjustment steps with feet, such as pivoting and patting footsteps through the court, exemplifies necessary quickness. However, court-sense is different from sheer movement. When players develop a razor-sharp sense for positioning and sprinting, intuitively grasping the area with precision, a subconscious awareness is cultivated regarding the court's space.

How do tennis players develop court-sense if they aren't endowed with it? This next eye-opening exercise involves using both baselines on the court. Diagrams are also presented which illustrate the following explanation:

Place markers, cones or even a pyramid of tennis balls in a parallel line to the baseline about 4 feet inside the court. Take note of the amount of space that exists between the baseline - to your line of markers or cones. Then, walk to the other side of the court. Stand at the baseline and note the stunning difference between the amount of space that you have just compared and the smaller amount of space you view from further away.

Why should this comparison increase your court-sense? As you set down the markers or cones, you probably noticed that you had a good deal of space. When you do this exercise, you will be amazed at the large amount of space you view from close proximity juxtaposed with the tiny amount of space you viewed from afar. This realization is a wonderful enhancer for increasing court-sense. The reality is that you have a great deal of space. It's probable due to earlier visual impressions that you assumed your previously struck shots landed adjacent to those markers, and landed just mere inches from the baseline. But after you do this exericse, you discover a generous 3-4 feet of space exists between those markers and the baseline.

Court Sense: Steps 1 and 2

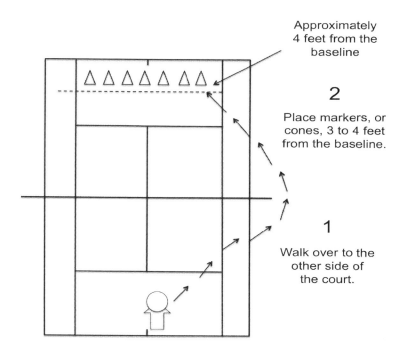

Approximately 4 feet from the baseline

2

Place markers, or cones, 3 to 4 feet from the baseline.

1

Walk over to the other side of the court.

Court Sense: Step 3

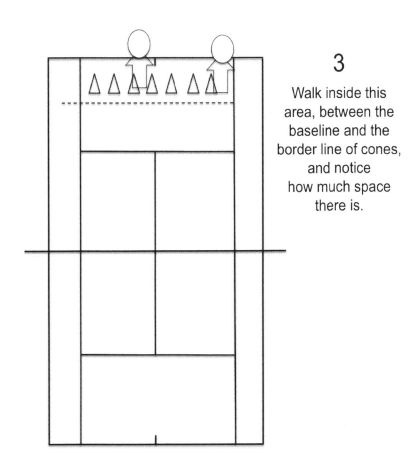

3

Walk inside this area, between the baseline and the border line of cones, and notice how much space there is.

Court Sense: Step 4

4

Walk back
to the
baseline,
to your
original side
of the court.

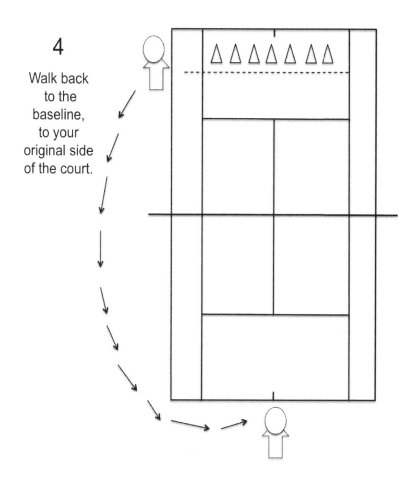

Court Sense: Step 5

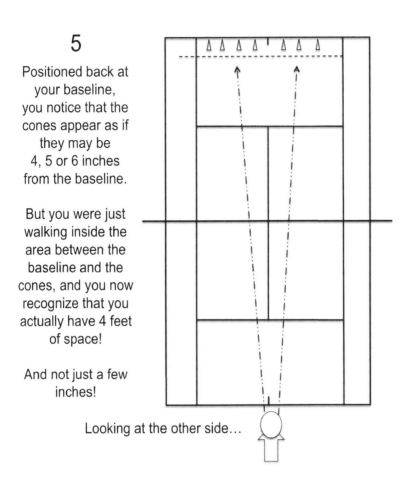

5

Positioned back at your baseline, you notice that the cones appear as if they may be 4, 5 or 6 inches from the baseline.

But you were just walking inside the area between the baseline and the cones, and you now recognize that you actually have 4 feet of space!

And not just a few inches!

Looking at the other side...

Place those markers or cones, inside the service lines and sidelines too. Your groundstrokes, volleys, overheads and return-of-serves will resonate with those spatial renditions you have developed from discerning the tennis court. When doing drills, you want to initially stand in one place. Afterwards, move over to stand a few feet from the center on another chosen place on the court and hit numerous balls, one after the next.

Venture to another area of the court, beginning another round of shots where your stationary position is distinctly identified. Get soundly acquainted with how the court appears, how the court looks to you from each region. A development of this strong spatial sensitivity of the court accompanied with agile movement leads singles and doubles players to inherit the uniqueness of court-sense.

Another useful exercise to examine the spaciousness of the court is to walk diagonally through it, re-gathering your newest tennis insights. Look at the other side of the court from where you are and draw an imaginary line indicating a place where you would like a shot to land from where you stand. A good spatial exercise is to note the line of a shot from its point of origin to its destination. Sprinting in diversified ways on the court is helpful. Most exercises involving court sprints are done on the baseline or sidelines. But players should also consider inventing a variety of sprints which have no uniformity and instead reflect the angles and diagonal movements players use. Exercising unstructured and randomized sprints enable players to simultaneously gain court-sense, footwork and speed.

Court-sense should never be underestimated because this spatial milieu underlies the magic behind all tennis players' talents. Time spent on the tennis court without ever swinging induces court-sense. An example relates to children who are introduced to tennis at very early ages. Children play, skip and hop in the area long before they ever even successfully strike the ball. Children experience the advantages of acquiring court-sense before understanding the game.

THE BASELINE AS A MEDIAN OF MEASURE

The precisional goal is to strike the ball perfectly inside the court due to an expanded spatial awareness. In order to achieve that special perception, tennis players must increase their intuitive assessment of the court, specifically the baseline. Players can strike balls for hours from all parts of the court yet forego the necessary focus that measures the various ranges of distance. This related concept was mentioned in the previous section, *The Relevance of Extra Space*.

The pursuit of territory outside the baseline bounds will be brand new to players who have never purposely endeavored to strike in this spacious area. Envision, if a player has never freely ventured beyond this boundary - the baseline - then it's impossible, literally impossible to precisely calculate or at least have a solid sense of where this baseline is situated in the breadth of that space. Everyone is familiar with the phrase, "Think outside of the box," yet asking players to experiment outside of the tennis court (the rectangular box) conjures such resistance. Basically, the innuendos are the same.

The foundation of this sport is grounded in precisional aim, consequently players enlighten their tennis acuity as they blend their concerted power with the expansive space near the baseline, an exploit which players must explore. The baseline is actually a *median of measurement* on behalf of space situated 1 foot in front of the baseline and space 1 foot behind the baseline. If players strike their shots to land in "the general area" near the baseline or sidelines, the system of developing precision is much slower compared to the veritable methodical manner regarding the median concept.

In other words, if a player has the ability to consistently strike the ball exactly 1 foot in and concurrently has the ability to strike the ball exactly 1 foot out, then this player has a keen sense of exactly where the baseline is situated. If a player has the ability to strike 8 for 10 balls, 1 foot outside the baseline, a good probability exists that this player has moreover developed a sensory regarding that adjacent space inside the baseline. Accordingly in practice, you should try to send the ball 1 foot outside of the baseline and then send 1 ball inside the baseline to indicate that you know exactly where the baseline is located *by your feel*.

Singles players should strike the ball deeply into the court. Doubles players may inquire if striking the ball near the baseline is valuable for their strategies. Any player capable of striking the baseline has developed the ability to strike the ball mightily through the court. Singles and doubles players must use the *entire tennis court* since it typifies the major expertise. Doubles and singles players who forego this focus give up their potential court expertise and power. This baseline skill exposes players' abilities regarding their spatial court measurements along with their inborn freedom to swing out when it becomes necessary.

The Baseline as a Median of Measure

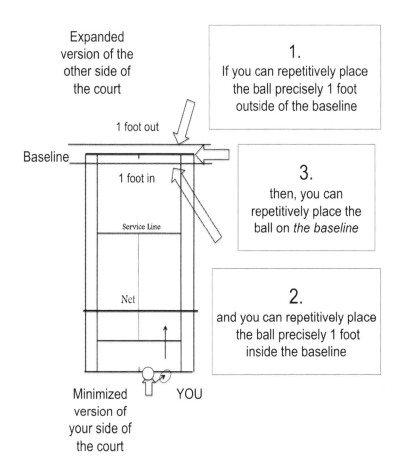

Expanded version of the other side of the court

1 foot out

Baseline

1 foot in

Service Line

Net

Minimized version of your side of the court

YOU

1.
If you can repetitively place the ball precisely 1 foot outside of the baseline

3.
then, you can repetitively place the ball on *the baseline*

2.
and you can repetitively place the ball precisely 1 foot inside the baseline

SAVVY SIDELINES

Tennis players may pleasurably experience a melodious impromptu when striking a court sideline. That sideline is such a skinny line, promising adulation when players strike it and mediocrity when they don't. Given this desired condition, the story of the sideline should be investigated more thoroughly. A task so enrapturing is worth much of a player's attention. This section concentrates on discovering the sideline that you never knew.

Earlier explanations exposed the roomy spaciousness of a newly discovered tennis court leading players to amplify their abilities. These ideas are also applied to sharpen sideline skills. How else do tennis players familiarize themselves with accurate distances from where they stand unless they aim into space adjacent to the sidelines? Using lateral space on the outside of the sidelines develops a sharp sense for the sideline itself. A singles or doubles player who intentionally strikes a ball 1 foot, 2 feet and 3 feet wide (implemented in practice sessions only) expands perception. Balls struck in space around the sideline gauge how well players perceive the area. When players strike clusters of cross-courts and down-the-lines, they should reach beyond the sideline to develop sideline awareness. The sideline, too, is a median of measure. The only difference between the baseline and the sideline, being regarded as a median, is that a player's perception is situated on the sideline fringe.

Hopefully, you have thoroughly interpreted this path that you have been on so far. Your foundation of facts, stats and your court perception will be soon overlapped with mental and creative themes. The Baseline T middle shot is extremely useful to steer you to eventually orchestrate a perfect "sideline" shot. A sideline shot depends on a direct, linear strike. This explains why the comprehension regarding the Baseline T is essential for your future precision.

Although players should vie for service box depth, the service box sidelines are relevant. Those sidelines are especially much more significant than designing complex strategies once players are immersed in the neutrality of the point. Since the serve is a major part of the game, players should develop their serves to the upmost limits by using the sidelines.

The unused areas in the service box give you the illusion that you have more service box space than is really available. Each service box is a rather narrowed, limited area where you place serves. As a ball travels further distances, further away from you, the area in front of you slims, narrows and becomes constricted. The service box suggests a certain type of optical illusion since you really want to use the depths and the sides of the box instead of the fore areas. In addition, players must know that the *feel* in their hands enhances sideline precision.

LET'S CHAT ABOUT CONFIDENCE

Confidence is typically defined as a self-governed belief in one's abilities. A player with confidence delivers magnificent talent in light of given situations. Many players tend to believe that confidence is a healthy, principal quality that they ought to maintain throughout their tennis matches. When players are offered advice likened with these notions, they should madly squint, fasten their belts, quickly pick up their tennis bags and flee. Confidence can be fleeting!

Have you experienced match situations where you "felt" confident followed by other matches slipping from your control? Confidence can be acknowledged as a wave of positive energy. Nevertheless, a rational player wonders how reliable confidence is. In tennis, confidence can have diversified meaning. Having expectations is an indication of displaying a "confident" mode where one player expects to win over another. Expectation utilized in this scenario portrays a player self-imposing rigorous motivation and demand on oneself. Confidence and expectation might be related although the conditions may also disparately branch apart.

Confidence also suggests that a player feels comfortable on the court, having spent hours on end practicing repetitive tennis skills. Comfort may translate to confidence but the absolute connotation of confidence remains inadequate. A poor presumption of confidence suggests that a player holds to fallacious notions of wished-for tennis faculties. At times, the idea of confidence can be a false replacement for some need. Arrogant or pompous attitudes portray behaviors occasionally mistaken for confidence. No player accomplishes substantiality on the tennis court with those attributes!

The real gems lay in courage, character and conviction. Tennis players who maintain courage, character and conviction, qualities earned through adversity and success, play as if they have a nice reservoir of confidence. A player who exclaims a need for confidence on the court is unknowingly in pursuit of courage, and character and conviction. It's obvious that players filled with ambitious desire become brave and hustle after important points. Although these players might harbor doubt about winning, they are willing to go all out, risking their full effort. These players could be uncertain about the possibility of winning, fearful, fighting through the fear, yet they are ready to embrace winning if it happens. These players parade tennis courage.

Character is established from hardships, failures, losses, and trial and error instead of sheer court wins. A tennis player with character is determined to win, unbending in desire and obstinate in will. A player formulates an internal statement of conviction craving to succeed from the ground of the heart.

The inference of confidence is an austere description that shrouds the real qualities of mental strength. To compete with courage, character and conviction is to radiate confidence. Self-reliance and self-assertiveness are more precise portrayals of what players really want and need instead of the intangible vastness of confidence. Above all, tennis players who have an intelligent strategy, a plan that can be unduly depended on, invite the attributes of confidence into their games naturally.

THE MENTAL TOUGHNESS TOOL

The bewitching quality of mental toughness is examined. Self-beliefs overshadow what players expect from their tennis performances and these self-impressions generally contrast the realities regarding how players actually operate.

A tennis player walks out onto a court with personal life experiences, armor and weakness tagging along. Tennis armor is a composite of features such as strength, clarity, courage, character and conviction. Weaknesses are fused with features such as disbelief, fear and a lack of faith in a purpose. A player could have doubt over a match's future outcome or might be distraught with nerves. Regardless, this condition with its broad spectrum reveals a player's propensity to be perfectly human.

Every tennis player holds a measure of fear that must be shuffled, shut out, conquered and eradicated if exuberant play is to ensue. Some tennis players are strained with falsified self-assumptions, believing they should march onto a tennis court with invulnerable, unwavering fearlessness. The truth is players can convert the energy of doubt and fear into a vibrant winning desire. When relegated to a helpless tennis state, even invoking the power of anger can potentially help alter a player's energy toward a positive state. Players do not need to be stuck in woes of fear and doubt on the court.

Former syntheses of both simple and complex formulas have proposed many ways to enhance mental tennis fortitude. Those methods range from being ultra-focused, to possessing a healthy attitude, to experiencing an abundance of happiness and peace on the tennis court. Are you wondering if these analogies and formulas would work at the hub of your mental alacrity? Alas, a player's mental toughness is never gauged through consistent, controlled or scientific methods on the court since several immeasurable factors are interconnected in tennis matches. A smart, reliable strategy *combined* with mental toughness is one example of a potent mix because one domain without the other would still lack a major tennis component. Mental-strength attributes will always propel players further than players who lack the quality.

The goal of sustained mental fortitude is for winning the majority of your tennis matches and to win those matches with supple ease. Let's examine the following example depicting a typical scenario of a player expressing mental toughness.

The first points of a match reveal a nervous or anxious player. Unusual mistakes probably occur which never occur in the regular course of a match. Adrenalin races, vision could be a bit obscured and the player could be short of breath. As the match proceeds to the 2nd game, nerves unravel and settle. This player begins to concentrate more intensely with a strategic plan. Self-generated mistakes and errors have barely any effect on the mood. This player refuses to become emotionally disconcerted when the opponent displays a sharp round of shots in a row. The possibilities are ignored that the match could potentially sway in the opponent's favor.

This player recognizes that numerous thoughts pervade the mind. Yet, this player also realizes that willpower can sway the match toward victory. The roughest debacle an opponent faces is a focused, assertive and persistent player and the tough player knows this.

Making sure you are emotionally relaxed, visualizing the happiness that you want to feel, enjoying the moment or perhaps attempting to associate tennis with a pastime joy, these blissful experiences may be perfect emotional settings for weddings or celebratory events, but these lovely modes of diminished battleground intensity are inappropriate for tennis competition. A player has the chance to relax and rejoice once the match has been won. If players feel countered by too many downbeat thoughts, rather than fight the negative, apply the *9 Dynamics for Tennis Toughness* found at the end of this section. Mental toughness involves the choice to prevail along with the decision to get rid of the negative.

Is this method exclusive, mentally muscling your way through a match? An amalgamation of techniques procures the condition to be mentally tough. Whether particular methods are better than others is a personal choice.

Variations of the formula must be mentioned alongside this initial presentation. Suitable emotional and sensory realms etch important roles in the mind game. If a player concentrates with a soulful, unconditional passion, then the overabundance of positive energy is powerful. Striving to compete in the elixir of the moment, *the zone*, and being overwhelmed with a sense of calm, tethered with concentration, is a highly commendable endeavor. Interestingly enough, methods of muscling mental toughness actually evoke elevated composure.

A word of counsel to the meek-hearted: players who are naturally passive should avoid suggestions that placate their passion. Subduing a passive tennis player puts a fighter's spirit to sleep. The reverse side of this situation is the aggressive impatient player who may need to contain feelings or control emotions to compete soundly. Tennis is a mentally aggressive sport and to suppress one of the verdant aspects of the game is unwise. The better option would be to refocus this aggressive player's effort, using that energy to face tennis situations with discipline.

A tough player consents to wonder, ready to repeatedly witness unimaginable tennis outcomes. A few errors from an opponent, along with a lucky shot or two streaming from the tough player's racquet, and the set could be won. If a set is lost, the mentally tough player might languish over the result for a moment. Although immediately, a tough player begins the 2nd or 3rd set renewed. Tennis players who lose their cool and get very upset should remember the only point that matters is the very last point of the match.

A player's mental state regarding wins and losses must be scrutinized. The realities of winning and losing prompt one another to reach greater heights. To thoroughly comprehend phenomena associated with mental toughness, a player needs to investigate the twofold side of this condition.

Do mentally tough players fear negative outcomes? The spirit of mental toughness honors risk. Players must recognize that a few points can determine the distinction between losing and winning. If a player experiences the burden of doubt and fear, courage is absent in that particular moment. Therefore, a player's prerequisite is to decide exactly how competition will be approached. Fear is present yet bravery is the goal. Tennis players who yearn to evoke their highest tennis demeanors should aspire to obtain a sharp-edged strategy and courage. Courage and fear ironically live together but as courage rises to the top, fear gets left behind.

One more significant theme hovers over the player's proclivity for being mentally tough. When players are equipped with a smart winning strategy, a mode they can depend on, they feel assured. Consequently, mental sturdiness naturally results. A player's level of mental toughness is frequently tied to a successful strategy and keen understanding of the game. Beyond question, a player's conscious decision that commits to excellence is the backbone sustaining mental toughness.

9 Dynamics for Tennis Toughness

1   Accept nervousness and imperfection

2   Concentrate intensely

3   Be austere with conduct

4   Evade being emotionally disconcerted
    no matter what circumstances befall

5   Ignore the negative

6   Be deliberate

7   Be assertive and persistent

8   Claim your willpower

9   Focus on a dependable strategic plan

WHAT'S LUCK GOT TO DO WITH IT?

The exponential tales about luck color the storybook of tennis. At times, "good luck" beholden to tennis players has been lightheartedly referred to as "divine intervention." The quality is so unique that few words are completely synonymous with the idiom in the English language. Players and spectators are aware when they witness luck at crucial, critical moments. Since competitive tennis treads the fine line between winning and losing, winners would be wise to humbly acknowledge its properties. The less fortunate player, who experiences dashes of good luck yet endures a loss, would be sensible to receive defeat with humility.

Propitious luck described in this book is notably different from the generalized random type. In a beguiling way, players should prepare to experience fortune on the court. Randomized luck is coincidental and unexpected, although a strategic and systematic preparation invites the providence a player needs. A player who consents to focus on serves and return-of-serves and strives to use the court's totality attracts the boon of luck. Sharpening one's mental toughness skills and applying analysis to matches summons godsend moments too. Luck depends on the orchestration of a multifarious approach.

Luck often leads to one player's victory and another's loss since the fine line between winning and losing can be the difference of a few points. When players win their matches, one could presume that luck occurred at unusual and abstruse moments. Good fortune might magically descend on players in moments when they really need the point, for which propitious luck is considered mysteriously delicate. This earned brand of fate is necessary for players' wins. Every tennis player should glisten with reverence when perfect luck is witnessed.

The upside of being mentally tough is having luck. Mental toughness relies on strategies to invoke the mystery. Tennis players should keep building their games by analyzing their match wins and losses. Losses, though unappealing to discuss, are valuable through introspection. Acknowledging where those tough moments lacked potency enables players to emerge emboldened the next time around. Given that winners receive satisfaction from the triumph, they should still consider foregoing full, bursting self-centered credit for their victories. Winners ought to always be grateful to an outlier, a coach, friends and certainly, luck.

Players who put their best efforts forward yet decline to dwell on their achievements compete with tennis humility. The humble player welcomes success, knowing luck participated in the outcome. Winning will occur more regularly if players take steps to invite the intangible into their tennis games.

Obviously, winners arrive home glorified with the day's success. But tomorrow is a new day and tennis wins relished yesterday no longer reside with the same intensity. Keep the ground ripe for your next matches. Tennis strategies combined with the quintessence of modesty are the superlative qualities behind a player's luck.

THE CONVICTION OF WINNING

The inclusive concept of winning is embedded deeply in the subconscious. People classified as "winners" are adulated and fittingly, tennis players admire those who win regularly. Players inquiring into the midst of their desires might ask; "How deeply do I want to win?" The broad populace assumes that everyone wants to win and nobody really wants to lose, right? To certify how a player feels, "How badly do I want to win?" is a question that tennis players should repeatedly ask themselves.

How established is your desire to win? Along a purview between 1 and 100, where do you rate your desire to win? This piercing inquiry implores to get to the bottom of your need. You probably believe that the general tennis playing populace intends to win 100% of the time. It might baffle you to know the answer is postponed, captivated in several tennis players' minds as they contemplate their need and desire to win. Sometimes instructors or coaches judge the importance of a multipart strategy and paltry technique as more appropriate versus applying a banal winning plan. One example points to the singles player who goes for broke on every shot by aiming 2 inches above the net or the doubles player who attempts a thunderous volley when all that was needed was to put the ball deep into the court. Prosaic strategies which tennis players are willing to use determine winning. Simply stated, players should endeavor to put the ball in the court one more time than their opponents as opposed to attempting outright winners. Players performing grand maneuvers fend against the grain of winning consistently.

When players use eminent strategies such as focusing on serves and return-of-serves, striking more shots through the court's center and using the court's spaciousness, it could be highly presumed that these same players cannot stand to lose. Chances are these players dislike losing with a passion and become internally distraught when they do lose. Logically, they forego any type of unpredictable play just to avoid losing. An opponent subconsciously or consciously senses a player's unnerving desire to win, configuring the nature of the fight.

Negatively-toned expressions such as, "I don't want to lose," are half-hearted compared to straightforward assertions such as, "I want to win" or "I intend to win." Positively toned statements launch the necessary affirmations that players must silently repeat to themselves prior to the competitive occasion. The winner reserves a moment to acknowledge and affirm the need, precisely targeting the will to win with a firm sense of purpose. Should all players develop a statement about wanting to win, reciting the referent? Strangely enough, without internal declarative statements, the match can be easily swayed from a player's fort. Without the strong firm avowal to win, the need has not been fully clarified. Players are sometimes unaware of their willful declarations before a match because the intentional tone is abstractly exercised.

Declare exactly what you want before you begin your match. Do you assume that your need to win surpasses the act to clarify your purpose? Regardless of form, the verity of your admission enhances your willpower and draws you directly towards the fulfillment of that goal on the tennis court.

Clinching the Points, Set and Match

Many of the sturdiest players have forged ahead only to watch the score shockingly undo itself like yarn rapidly unravel from its spool. Today's players contend with the additional accent of speed, formerly absent in the combative tennis arena. Technological power enables players to display tremendous shots, allowing for great unpredictability from opponents. Have you ever been ahead, 5-1 or 5-2, lost the set and wondered what happened? Did you construe explanations why you lost the set or why an opponent overcame the score's deficit? Either way, this discussion plunges to the root of the issue, illustrating *when* to clinch significant points in the game.

In the past, players fought for every point and they put fierce pressure on the opponents. Applying aggressive pressure reflected the emotional and psychological brawn tennis players prided themselves on. The mental aspects triumphed over the game contrary to the divergence that focuses today on power. Crushing serves and return-of-serves have transformed tactics and for this reason, players must bear down on these crucial features.

Each point is important though players may disprove of using their intense energy to fight fiercely. Players get wiped out from previous points, become fatigued, the wind changes the matches' momentum and other times the score triggers a loss of concentration. Despite these situations, players should attempt to fight relentlessly for every point. Fighting can also suggest different connotations. Some players believe that they ferociously fight by roughly swiping at the ball. This outward physical overtone greatly differs from the tacit meaning of fighting fervently.

"Letting up" is a phrase used to describe those moments when players feel convinced that the set or match is tucked away neatly inside their pocket. Consequently, these players feel that they can afford to loosen and lighten up. These players perceive their intense concentration is less necessary in view of the fact that the victory is close at hand. This relinquishment is essentially the biggest blunder a tennis player can make. When players feel aplomb with assurance about their soon-to-be win, a high likelihood exists that their win could wobble out of their hands. In the attempt to stop the wobble, a dash of panic emerges and tightness pervades limbs, joints and breathing. Disbelief that the lead has been lost and slipped from their fingertips, players begin to miss shots never before missed and mistakes haphazardly crop up. A player finds it insurmountable to create those previously successful strikes. The entire shot selection which built up the score's lead, collapsed. A player who was winning now feels the opponent dominates with a foot on the gas pedal. The worried player desperately wants to halt the opponent's momentum and feels helpless in the back-trot. Bleak thoughts fly through the player's mind, "Oh no, I am losing. Moments ago I was winning so easily! How do I retrieve my command, my control, my lead? This set was in the palm of my hand! What is happening? Why and how did my opponent suddenly become stronger both physically and mentally?" Frantic rattling occurs when a player has owned the match and lets it go. Inconsolably, the player who lost assumes complete accountability for losing the match.

The good news extrapolated from this situation is that both competitors, player and opponent, acted together like an inexplicable combustion of energies. Both singles players and doubles teams coalesced to create that harrowing effect akin to falling from the sky without a parachute. How do you ascertain this scenario will be avoided on a regular basis? The stark issue of players letting up must be addressed. Before the discussion proceeds, the incontestable spotlight on serves and return-of-serves is recapped. Those serves and returns potentially place 60%-70% of the match back on track. Now let's revert back to the issue of letting up.

When you are ahead 40-0 or 40-15 in the game, this is the last place to reminisce about the lead or experiment with unique shots that you are unaccustomed to winning points from. Many players appreciate the 3 point lead within a game though they assume 2 points could be let go and they are still in the lead, as the score twiddles down from 40-0 to 40-30. Never treat the score in this mundane manner! Any instance where a player prevails with a 3 point or 2 point lead, those points must be secured. A sharp seasoned player recognizes the opportunity to finalize the game and gets into gear to step up to the moment. At this phase, the game is almost won and the player needs only 1 point.

In the ominous scenario, the player who was culpable for letting up supported a falsified assumption. This player (who was winning) presupposed that the opponent (who was losing) must have been despondent and forlorn via the scoreboard.

The player mistakenly believed how difficult it would be for the opponent to climb from the score's deficit. Players should never presuppose that the effort required for their opponents to fight has been abandoned. Players strolling ahead may portentously assume opponents will basically let up and allow them to win. These notions chuck every noble strategy to the beleaguering wind. Players must never assume that they know the mental or emotional state of an opponent until the match is over.

THE LITTLE ITEMS ARE REALLY BIG ITEMS

The significant force in tennis competition is the serve which begins each point with its *defining* toss. Service motions rely on the auxiliary function of the ball toss. Circumstances regarding the silent toss mislead players to assume it plays an inconsequential role. However, the toss can dictate the service's fate. Contrary to how the toss is viewed, a player's exclusive control to release the ball should be perceived as an advantage. Players reserve various options with the toss such as remaining utterly still before beginning the serve. The service toss and the serve itself are the only motions where players are completely free from being wrenched out of their position. Servers retain command with the self-issued serve as players need not chase balls around the court. Paradoxically, many players disregard the tossing arm that controls and provides this principal task.

A player's back, shoulders, arms and hands are sturdy functions for both the serve and ball toss. Each tennis player has an individualized tendency to move in distinct rhythms and to naturally sway in accordance to the individual body type. Consequently, instructional advice for striking serves varies for each person. The ball toss is a small, brief motion lasting a bit more than one second. No matter which type of service motion a player chooses to use, the ball toss is a skill of smoothness, stillness and delicacy.

The fingers that place the ball toss are decisive controls. Make sure all five fingers grip the ball with light pressure and the hand retains its agility. Imagine placing the ball toss with stillness, similar to the way the golf tee sets the golf ball. An amazing similarity exists between the tennis ball toss and the golf tee structure. The difference is that the ball leaves the hand before the strike. Fingers support and propel the ball into alignment. Vision should follow the vertical line the moment the ball leaves your fingers. Long-lasting vision affixed to the ball rising above a player's head is another little item that's really a big item.

Aligning the arm with the verticalness of the body can be practiced by standing next to a wall, court fence or backdrop. The reason that players should do this wall exercise is because servers usually believe that their tossing arm is fully extended. This marks the difference between how servers feel that their tossing arm is aligned versus where the arm actually is.

This instruction requests that the player targets attention to the 5th finger of the ball tossing hand. That little finger plays an exacting role. The 5th finger, which pulls and extends when the ball has left the hand and suspends in the air, sets up other areas of alignment in the arm, shoulder and neck. If a player stretches the ball toss arm perpendicular to the sky, the 5th finger can perfect the alignment of the shoulder, arm and hand, so the service motion carries out the utmost stretch.

The final illumination about the ball tossing action is about the subtle placement of the ball in mid air. Flexibility of the arm is influential for smoothness and extension. As the ball rises above one's height, a player can choose attributes such as placing the ball toss to the right, the left or straight above the head. Other options include placing the ball lower (in the wind), higher (indoors), or out in front or behind where the server will strike the serve. Ideally, a player wants a full vertical extension when the serve is struck.

A progressive approach regarding the toss and serve has recently emerged. It requires the acceleration of both arms, about 3/4ths on the way up prior to releasing the ball. In one rhythmic moment, the actual release of the ball and the swing are formed simultaneously. The ball toss is struck during this continuous quickened movement. This speedier motion propels more vigor into the strike and stabilizes the ball in the wind.

The Service Toss Arm

Correct:

Stand next to a vertical structure, such as a wall or a door.

Align your tossing arm and your shoulder adjacent to the structure.

Feel the straight up position that your arm needs to maintain when you will eventually place the ball toss in the air.

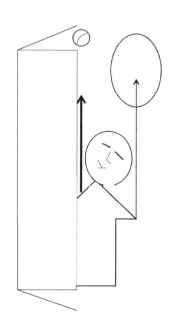

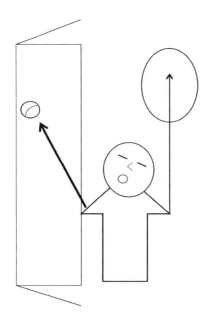

Less Correct:

A slanted tossing arm is
not aligned with the
vertical structure.

INSIDE-OUT FOREHANDS

The inside-out forehand is the zenith of a singles and doubles tennis player's creations. Imagine for a moment that the court changes its locality and diagonally shifts. This imagery of a shifting court is comparable to the angles a player creates, swiveling shots outside sideline bounds. If the player is right-handed, the inside-out forehand replicates a similar ball curve of a left-hander striking the same forehand. The right-hander instantly becomes a lefty whereas the lefty becomes a right-hander for one short moment where players irrefutably take on each other's traits.

To prepare for the inside-out forehand, players move around their backhand to strike an undulating forehand. Players can strike the ball to land deep in the right-hand or left-hand corner of the opponent's court. This angled shot curves away from the sidelines or the alleys after it bounces. It veers out of the court differently than the customary cross-court forehand. Inside-out forehands manifest into sidespin, curves and spirals.

Contrary to inside-out forehands, cross-court forehands resume a linear path. Angles are straighter from the striking point since depth is a cross-court strength. No matter which hand-dominant a player might be, both inside-out forehands and cross-court forehands produce laudable effects for singles and doubles opponents to utilize sharp angles.

Practice inside-out forehands with the intention to land the ball inside the court's ideal sweet spot where the service line and the sideline meet. Each inside-out forehand you strike depends and varies decidedly on several factors: where you are positioned on the court, the speed of the oncoming ball and how high or low you strike the ball. Other adjustments that you have to do with are measuring distances and angles, along with striking the ball at its apex, or on the rise, or when the ball has dipped low.

Inside-Out Forehand, Right-hander

Singles

3 effective places
to strike your inside-out forehands

And vice versa:

A player should become alert early in a match when recognizing that the opponent is capable of striking inside-out forehands.

Consequently, singles players on the receiving end of right-hander inside-out forehands will be able to anticipate the ball's trajectory and angle.

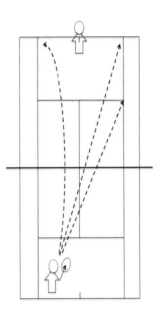

Inside-Out Forehand, Left-hander

Doubles

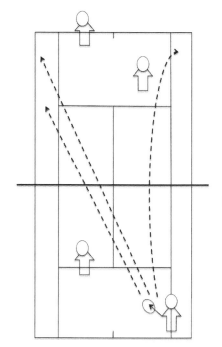

3 effective places
to strike your inside-out
forehands

And vice versa:

Doubles players should become alert early in a match when they recognize that their opponents are capable of striking inside-out forehands.

Consequently, doubles players on the receiving end of left-hander inside-out forehands will be able to anticipate the ball's trajectory and angle.

Since right-handed people outnumber the amount of left-handed people, when a right-hander player encounters a lefty, the adaptation presents an atypical challenge. One of the only apparent disadvantages of being a lefty in tennis is that fewer left-handed players exist to instruct their own kind. Visual examples are extremely helpful while learning a tactile textural sport, giving right-handers this developmental advantage.

Players can be introduced to techniques on how to strike an inside-out forehand yet elaborate instructional words may lack expeditious results. To begin with, the inside-out forehand is a mechanism altogether different from how many players are accustomed to approach the ball. Inside-out forehands require players to move around their backhands with agile footwork. An inside-out forehand is resplendent with extra hand motion and a loosened wrist. Inside-out forehands have emphasis on angle and spin. The quickest method to learn how to create sharp-angled inside-out forehands is to experiment by hitting the ball onto the outer court sidelines. Singles players should purposely strike their inside-out forehands inside the doubles alleys. Doubles players should replicate the same procedure and strike their shots to land outside of the doubles alleys. Expanding court boundaries develops players' abilities to freely swing near the sideline's width.

If players are able to purposely strike the ball to land 3 or 4 feet wide, how demanding can it be to bring the ball in a little closer reducing some pace from the strike? A player can learn techniques all day long but if the player exaggerates the method, the skill is learned faster. The fear of missing shots "out" inhibits a player to genuinely learn how to pursue many skills.

Opening Up the Inside-Out Forehand

Singles

The best way to
learn to open up an
inside-out forehand
(in practice)
is to freely explore
the region
around the sideline!

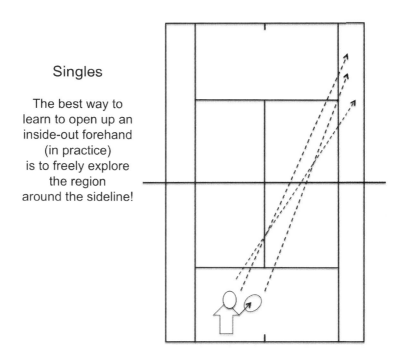

THE SWINGING VOLLEY PROJECT

The tennis culture finally acknowledges swinging volleys as conventional shots only after decades of conflicting views. A misunderstanding over the swinging volley has forever hovered over the tennis panorama. To clarify the discrepancy, the volley should be defined before addressing the swinging volley. The definition of a volley asserts that a volley is a ball struck in mid air before the bounce. The classic volley is simple, relying on hand skill and a constant ready position. "Less is better" is good instructional advice for the short-punched classic volley.

Volleys have been transitional from striking the ball with a tightened short punch to a variety of punches involving added shoulder motion. The hottest "volley" is presently the swinging volley. Swinging volleys are executed everywhere on the tennis court. Once upon a time, tennis players who took swings at volleys were told that their volleys were hideously incorrect. Many people still go aghast when told it's legitimate to swing at their volleys. The remnants of resistance have prevailed despite the swinging volley's acceptance into the mainstream. To let you in on a secret, this maneuver has been emphatically used for decades. It's merely the designated title of "swinging volley" which is new.

This illegitimate swinging shot was dreadful for serve-and-volley players and rightfully so. Power has skyrocketed tennis performance. Speed has demanded that the mechanical technique correlate with 21st century tennis. Formerly, players charged the net after producing a stunning serve and sharply short-punching a volley for a winner. Volleyers had to arrive speedily to the net to punch the shot. Today, the tactic can be unpredictable and unmanageable since return-of-serves come wheeling into the court with almost as much power as serves fly over the net. Secondly, physical exercise is a focus of many people's regimen leading players in this era to be more athletic.

The swinging volley has incurred an eclectic connotation. It possesses the word "volley" which insinuates that the shot is a short punched motion without any prior swinging, performed only at the net. But the swinging volley is executed anywhere on the court by both singles and doubles players. In fact, the real swinging volley is a forehand or backhand struck in mid air before the ball bounces. Taken often in no-man's land or while progressing towards the net, it's also perfectly legitimate to hit the swinging volley when positioned at the net.

To create a swinging volley, take a groundstroke swing at a ball in mid air. This ball is usually a high sitter referred to as a floater. The floater is exactly what it implies, a ball floating at lower speeds. A player can instigate the swinging volley by preparing the court field with a lob. If a player sends over a high topspin lob or floater to an opponent, it's predictable that the return comes back nearly as high as it departed. In most circumstances, an opponent will attempt to bring the shot's height back down. Since the opponent will have some difficulty striking the higher bounce, the shot will probably fly back higher than intended or expected, floating back into the court. The opponent sends back this floater hence a swinging volley awaits in the wings. Or, a player might run an opponent off the court and as the player watches the opponent scamper and struggle to strike the shot, the player anticipates the ball will pop up. At that moment, the player makes a dash from the baseline, moves a few steps into no man's land and lingers in final anticipation to pummel the silver-lining swinging volley.

When adults initially learn the forehand and backhand, if the swinging volley is also taught, it becomes incorporated into players' styles naturally. When the swinging volley is presented after a player has played for many years, inserting this extreme and implacable stroke into one's stock of shots is somewhat challenging. A player situates at the baseline and complacently rallies with forehands and backhands. To hit the swinging volley well, the mind must change gears. Swinging volleys have the *aggressive attacking mindset of a serve-and-volley player*. This player aggressively shifts to attack the ball before it bounces. Since the swinging volley is different from the customary shot, this skill should be taught promptly otherwise attempting this rare shot feels like going against the adage of old-fashioned tennis. Regardless over this skill's intricacy, every player ought to be knowledgeable about the swinging volley.

Everyone must at least try the swinging volley given its efficacious role in a player's progression. Taking the ball in the air is instructive, teaching a player to swing at the ball before the bounce. The customary way to hit the groundstroke is to allow the ball to bounce, pop up then strike. By introducing the swinging volley, a player watches the ball in flight with as much concentration as watching the ball after the bounce. Measuring the ball flight before the bounce is unparalleled to measuring after its bounce. Executing a swinging volley leads players to approach the ball in flight without restraint. This skill prompts alertness for each and every ball during flight, characterizing the fundamental gift of anticipation.

The forehand and backhand (one-handed) both possess a moderate range of freedom, allowing players to be nimble. A loosened wrist is used. The two-handed backhand fares as well as the forehand for the swinging volley. If the body is unable to get around the ball fast enough, a player might move around the backhand and take a forehand swinging volley instead. If net players feel that swinging with two hands would be more effective than using one hand, they should go ahead and swing freely.

The swinging drop-volley is the shot of pure expertise. From the swinging volley preparation, a player can misleadingly issue a delicate slice in place of the robust swing. The swing begins from a floater inside no man's land and ends as a drop-volley. This exquisite motion feints an aggressive beginning and fades with a slice. This innovation barely passes over the net. The beauty of modern tennis is in its inventiveness along with the riddance of conventional technique.

SPINS UP, OFF AND AWAY

In the world of tennis power, spin is secondary, however spin creates bountiful opportunities. Topspins, side-spins, and under-spins compose the family of spin. Not every shot needs to unfurl into a power-loaded shot. Nor are all shots relegated to travel to the baseline and sidelines. However, the player who pursues full court usage will always hold the best proposal for winning.

Tennis is artistry, a place to combine shots with physical movements, intelligence and mental toughness. Although players must document opponents' strengths and weaknesses, an indifference regarding these weaknesses is mostly a result of rapid ball travel. Many players apathetically consider their opponent's reactions when giving opponents spin. In the rush of retrievals, tennis players neglect to analyze where opponents breakdown. Inquiring into opponents' weaknesses, players can tailor their tennis strategies in order to tackle their opponent's vulnerabilities. This method also allows players to display their own strengths.

For instance, you have an opponent who strikes the ball nicely when situated in one place though when the ball spins roughly to the right sideline, your opponent's timing lapses. With this data, you send a spin serve or a sidespin shot near that right sideline to disrupt your opponent's comfort zone. Instructional lessons should forego particularized emphasis on stroke production. In this case, the real accent should be placed on the spin itself. By learning various spins, a player's game is embellished with creativity and surprise.

Since the serve is the main builder of a point, spin is a good ally. The further away a ball toss is placed to the side, the more the player can slice the side of the ball to create a spin serve. This method follows a different technical procedure than other service motions. The spin serve is considered secondary or applied sparingly. Despite its lesser appeal, players struggle to control spin when it speedily swivels out of the service box. Strategy predicates on hitting serves deep. Yet, the spin serve which lands close to the sideline and possibly short furnishes an unforeseen effect.

A serve is both a smash and a short shot that arrives halfway into the court. If a ball travels *directly toward you* at 50 mph, 60 mph or 80 mph, you stand in its path with a higher chance of returning the ball. And vice versa. If your opponents stand in the path of your serve, it's highly probable they will deflect the ball back into play. Conversely, a returner has more difficulty when balls spin quickly outside of the court. Players can never sprint or race with parallel speeds alongside the ball's path.

On the flip side of this coin, if you encounter a spin serve as a returner, you must cut off the angle as you observe the ball's curved trajectory. In the event which you notice that your opponents are using spin, whether in serves or strokes, take a step inside the baseline and move forward to cut off the spin. Taking this step or two closer enables you to dock that spin's angle. A cardinal rule for players is that they should always move closer inside the court to lessen the spin-angle effect. Whether you are playing singles or doubles, all players should stop the curve from whisking them off the court.

The spin serve does not need to land on the sideline. Wherever the serve lands in the service box, the spin behaves as if it lands on the sideline, spiraling off the court. One of the sublime values of spin serves is that opponents become hard-pressed to react to the diversity players create.

If a server reproduces each serve uniformly flat, the returner never needs to adjust for a difference. The returner is free from worry at being surprised. On the contrary, a spin serve pushes an opponent off to the side of the court, opening a large remainder of the court. The spin mechanism jumbles the returners calculated and anticipated rhythms. Spin allows the server creative choices with forthcoming shots. Once the returner stands outside of the court sideline, the ball struck should go to the furthest corner of the court, right? Whether playing singles or doubles, an open court is an open court. And this first-ball-strike is the most innovative play. It demonstrates the chance to use your power shots. But, you must always ask whether this play is the best one for you due to the risk factor.

Back to the subject of spin. If a player has never learned to hit spins, the player should really first experiment with the exercise without expecting successful results inside the court. To learn how a ball spins sideways, how to create sidespin, take a ball in one hand and hold the racquet in the other as if you are going to create the lightest, softest forehand. Imagine the numbers of a clock placed on the face of the ball. Vertically brush the right side of the ball (for right-handed players) or the left side of the ball (for left-handed players). If the tennis ball is a clock, brush 3 o'clock on the yellow sphere. This racquet-head movement brushes 2 to 3 feet in an upward motion.

To learn how the ball spins with topspin, again take the ball in one hand and hold the racquet in the other as if you are to create the lightest forehand again. Vertically brush the side of the ball that faces you. The racquet-head movement should brush 2 to 3 feet in an upward motion.

For backspin, take the ball in one hand and hold the racquet-head high above the ball in the other hand. Vertically approach the mid backside of the ball with the racquet. Brush the sphere at 6 o'clock. The racquet-head movement should brush 2-3 feet in distance underneath the ball.

The creativity of slices, drop shots, chops, spin serves and topspin shots has all origins in spin. Once players truly understand how balls spin initiated from their racquet angles, they are ready to put these spinning forms into action. First practice spinning the ball in various ways *without intending to send the ball over the net* nor into the court. You will discover how to create spin and manage it into your serves and other parts of your game.

On windy days, the breeze thrusts a player's spins to the far corners of a court's terrain. The wind impels spin, especially if a player uses the wind according to the direction in which it blows. Players must know that when encountering wind, using any type of spin is advantageous. Wind splendidly assists spin which leads you to the next section, *The Wind Factor*.

THE WIND FACTOR

Topspins, sidespins, and under-spins struck in the wind are considered a coup de grace since wind compliments spin in tennis. All singles and doubles players should strive to be thoroughly familiar about their benefits in the wind. If a player is knowledgeable about playing with the wind and against the wind, this player can win easy and foreseeable points. A sky racing with clouds could upset an opponent's rhythm. Some players regard wind as an irritant and a drawback. Seasoned tennis players consider the wind a buoyant occasion to receive resplendent advantages. The geographical vicinity determines the type of wind patterns that players encounter when playing outdoors. Players must be sharply aware of the wind direction, the gusts and the velocities. True tennis champions are skillful masters of wind. These players are equipped with adaptability, using the capricious wind personalities of the day.

The perfect symmetry of the tennis court is altered when playing with the wind and against the wind. When players feel the force of wind blowing behind their back, the wind leads hence players play with the wind. Shots blowing with the wind's lead take arching bounces, awkward twists and curves. With the wind blowing behind a player's back, shots spring quickly off the racquet-head. Swinging will necessitate more controlled effort with a light touch. With the wind, a player should deflect an opponent's power and redirect those deflections.

When adding topspin, a player should carefully lift and aim the ball a few feet over the net. The ball will travel further into the back portions of the court when it bounces. It will kick up higher than when unaided by the wind's assistance. High topspin shots are magnificent since the ball gains velocity from the wind. The added topspin forces an opponent to work 2 and 3 times harder than if the wind had been absent. With the wind behind a player's back, angles zoom out of the court faster than without the wind's help, causing an opponent to scramble. Forehands and backhands struck with sidespin are extremely effective for the same reason. With the wind's help, shots that have spin, speed and angle are armored. Sidespin and topspin serves control the scene in this windy condition.

When players feel wind blowing against their body, they compete against the wind current. Against the wind, shots continually fight the wind current and are stopped short of what players would have intended. A player's shots heave backward, especially after those shots have landed on an opponent's side. A player who swings with tremendous force finds it difficult to send the ball "out." Adding topspin permits a player to swing even harder and keep the ball inside the court. Players should make sure to swing upward as the wind expectedly downward spirals the shot quickly into the lower part of the net. Against the wind, all downward motions should be avoided. Return-of-serves should be aimed through the court's center or aimed opposite of the crosswind. The force will unpredictably swerve the shot so returners need insurance that their return-of-serves retract into the court.

The highlights when playing against the wind are the utilization of under-spins, consisting of slices, drop-shots and chops. A short slice behaves similarly to a drop-shot. The wind stops its speed and stunts its travel. A drop-shot struck against the wind must be struck with vigor. The effect of this drop-shot will still produce a stunted shot that drops and halts. Lobs must be swung with a lot of force and height. Players should make sure that lobs have enough brawn to travel the full length of the court through grueling wind. Short lobs against the wind are never advised. A short lob will inevitably land even shorter in the court than players imagine. The short lob sits motionless inside the court, giving opponents the liberty to do whatever they please with its immobility. Serves and return-of-serves against the wind must be aimed 2, 3 and even 4 feet higher over the net than normal. Playing against the wind pulls the ball downward when hitting serves and return-of-serves.

The wind has gust patterns where it stops then picks up intensity again. This requires that a player attune to the wind's alternating manner. Players should be alert about the changing wind *the second before striking each shot*. Players who enjoy their days competing outdoors should know about stroking with and against the wind. Adjusting the speed on swings, using particular heights above the net, paying attention to the wind gusts and throwing in various spins reflect the art of playing tennis in the breeze.

OVERHEADS AND SMASHES

By this stage you have probably surmised the overhead and the service motion are identical and the only big difference is in the ball toss for the serve. Every chance you have to take an overhead, whether you are a singles or doubles player, seize it because it's a natural smash. The serve is considered a type of smash since it enters the court from a zenith point from above. The theme of smashing the ball is popular, replacing the long drawn-out groundstroke of the past. Former instructional rhetoric regarding groundstrokes emphasized the racquet-head movement, "low to high." Although still existent, this stroke has morphed into a stylish shot which has the racquet-face move across and on top of the ball. These forehands and backhands are considered smashing types of groundstrokes.

Power has limited the lob's usage, therefore a player might miss more overheads as less opportunities are available to strike it. The worse results which players want are overheads that sail directly into the net. Overheads are frequently missed because players assume they should aim downward and then aiming downward too early, the ball reels into the net. The overhead should be aimed upward on the ball, similar to the service motion. The overhead is equivalent to a serve except the overhead has the freedom to land anywhere in the spacious court. The overhead isn't limited to the restrictive area of the service box. Despite the overhead having free reign, it fails to carry the same statistical importance of a serve. Regardless, players must seize every opportunity to strike an overhead. Overheads are smashes descending into the court with more vertical force than any forehand or backhand ever incur. If the overhead has been a rarity in your game, it may be time to bountifully add it to your collection of shots. The overhead, akin to the serve, furnishes tennis players with an easy way to win points.

Another key error, besides sinking an overhead to the bottom of the net, occurs when players attempt to sharply aim their overhead to the far corners of the court. This aesthetically aimed shot is a potentially "easy point" turned into an "error waiting to happen." An overhead aimed directly toward the sideline is risky and unnecessary. Overheads vertically zoom downward. Their effectiveness comes from the forcefulness of the vertical quality. Vertical flight and force are good enough to win the point. Why should players push their luck with this 3rd riskier feature, going for sidelines and making their overheads more complicated with higher chances to err? Precautionary measures are necessary when a player's aim is subjected to extra speed, power and angle. Being prudent and making sure to put the overhead in the court instead of hitting it wide or into the net is a reasonable expectation since vertical flight and force already operate to their fullest. A fine place to aim an overhead with full potency is deep and directly through the court's center. In fact, unless overheads are practiced in mass production, players could find it difficult to repeatedly strike an overhead "out" from one baseline to the other. In practice, players should pursue launching their overheads beyond the baseline to develop power and a dexterous motion. Aiming overheads outside the region of the baseline is challenging.

Players should never hesitate when smashing overheads from the backend of the court.

If a player must aim for the sidelines, a substantial amount of room is available revealing the fundamental concept of tennis court spaciousness. However, a player must be aware of the courts' distances too. The further that a ball travels from a player, the sideline widths are further away, so they have narrowed. The closer a tennis player is situated to the width, the wider the court appears and it's easier to keep the ball within those sidelines. The further away the widths are located from the player, the more trying is the skill to keep the ball within the confines of the lines, requiring deft precision.

The overhead uses much space in flight. An overhead struck from the baseline is really an extended serve that freely travels 70 to 80 feet. If a player aims extraordinarily high over the net, for example at 5 or 6 feet, the height allows the player to strike the overhead with ease. Generating pace and distance are rooted in using heights over the net. If you attempt to strike overheads which adopt a net clearance by 5 or 6 feet, you realize how much court is available. Chances are that if you strike an overhead aimed high over the net with full potency, it goes deep and your opponent will have difficulty returning it. Although if your overhead sails low over the net, it will most likely land short, enabling your opponent to deflect the power and pop the ball back into the court.

Unloading overheads higher over the net and ignoring where your opponents are positioned is a smart plan. Doubles players often worry too much about their opponents instead of preparing to move and hit the best overheads possible. If your opponents stand still in one place, that's actually better for you because they shouldn't be standing still anywhere on the court. Likewise, you too should be constantly mobile, patting your footsteps side-to-side, up and back, ready to sprint. Players remaining loyal to one location and waiting for the balls to sail nearby, relinquish court authority. Singles and doubles players should be agile before the point begins.

Overheads are highly effective due to their hovering forcefulness that disbands the point. Instead of waiting for a lob to fly over, smart players instigate the opportunity to hit an overhead by sending over a lob or a sharp angle. These players are hoping that another lob follows their lobbing cue and that their opponent(s) will inadvertently flip up the ball high into the air.

To strike an overhead well, keep your body straightened and upright. Reach your other free arm vertically to the sky. Do this first before you close in near the ball. Quickly shuffle your footwork. Move underneath where you believe you will strike the ball at its apex. Squat with a straightened torso if you must, if the lob you receive is lower than your fullest potential reach. When lobs bounce higher than your extended racquet-head reach, keep your torso stretched to hit the overhead.

Do you recall the significance of the service ball toss? That free arm, straightened and extended, resembling a golf tee must align underneath the peak, the zenith where you will strike your overhead. Players should avoid measuring the travel of the ball with an arm that sways up and down while preparing to hit the ball. In other words, players do not want the arm moving while simultaneously assessing where the apex of the overhead will be struck. A player's vision finds the apex of the pending overhead and the feet move the body into alignment. The free arm and shoulder are lightly locked, straightening the moment the player realizes the shot is an overhead. Overheads are about the organizational set up.

Be prescient with your intent to create overheads. Every chance where you find the opportunity to take this governing shot, go for it!

A LADDER OF HEIGHTS

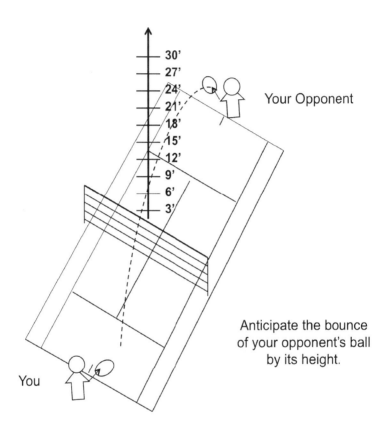

Your Opponent

Anticipate the bounce
of your opponent's ball
by its height.

You

Estimating where one's opponents will strike the ball should be of main importance for singles and doubles players. A major miscalculation results when players measure the ball's velocity and its destined landing after it crosses the net. These players' calculations occur too late. That ball should be watched as it lifts from the opponent's racquet from the other side of the net.

The crest over the net combined with degrees of power, angle and spin determine where your opponent's ball lands. To attain a preview where the ball is destined to cross the net, observe the lift from the opponent's racquet at that precise second the ball is struck. Players who estimate the probability regarding where the ball crosses the net early in an opponent's strike anticipate where the ball will land. In other words, a player who follows the ball's departure senses where the ball will bounce according to the height it crosses above the net.

This anticipatory skill appears exaggerated to players who have never been led to "read" their opponent's departing ball. Without applying this method, the ball's placement can take you by surprise. If you have never watched the ball leave your opponent's racquet, unnecessary winners have most likely startled you. The surprise received from opponent's offensive shots is seldom understood until anticipation is experienced. Once a player applies anticipation, control will be appended to the strike, extra time is gained and balance improves. A player who disregards the opponent's ball departure plays defensively. The player who watches the ball depart from the opponent's racquet plays offensively with sharper calculation. Why should you be disconcerted by what your opponents will attempt when you hold a preview? The necessity to exercise anticipation then becomes obvious.

Let's view the flip side of the measurement process. This "height" topic is a basic component though it's astonishingly overlooked. As players measure the heights of their opponent's shots, they should also be discerning the heights over the net regarding their own shots. Singles and doubles players need to develop an apt awareness of their own ball heights.

Discerning the Heights Over the Net

Regarding Your Own Shots

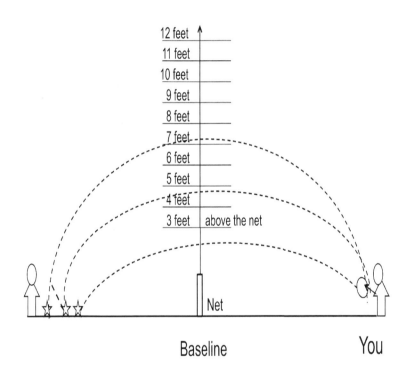

Tennis may be played for an entire lifetime yet players may never have realized that with each of their strikes, they've been subconsciously measuring the court's center. The specific area where the ball lands is a product of where the ball crosses the net with its fitting speeds, spins and angles. The summit of the ball's flight over the net and the destined landing of that ball perform together like a team. Your perception and control will be greatly enhanced when you measure the height where the ball clears the net.

The distance from one baseline to the other baseline is 78 feet. A player positioned 2 feet behind the baseline on one side of the court aims to the other baseline so the shot travels 80 feet. If a player chooses a spot 3 or 4 feet over the net and aims with a regulated amount of power and spin, the shot's destiny has been created. Rather than aiming 80 feet away, why not aim at a place above the net 40 feet away? How much easier a player can judge 40 feet of distance. If a player is given the choice to strike a target from 80 feet away or 40 feet away, which target is going to be easier to hit? A player's sense of measurement is never limited to the space confined within the court lines.

Players aware of heights and midpoints examine their shots and begin to analyze why certain shots "act" as they do. This contrasts players who are unaware that the midpoint of the court is constantly being measured. Too much power, reduced spin or too low over the net (the factor which usually constitutes the main accumulation of errors) place players on the defense. These red lights indicate an instant adjustment to a player's shots. Without this forewarning, players are prone to create the same shots over again with the same results.

For instance, choose a particular place - 3 feet over the net - and measure the speed and spin of the ball. Observe where your ball crosses the net and where it lands. You have superbly inherited a new quality about your own aptitude. You find that you are more precise when you measure a target on the court closer to where you are located. Players are notably recompensed by this contained sense of measurement while in motion.

Midpoint Concept

Instead of attempting to aim
80 feet away to the
baseline...

Choose a point 40 feet away
over the net,
from where you are,
for the same baseline shot.

Net

78 feet: Baseline

Players must know that a ball travelling 1 foot over the net falters to reach the baseline depths. Shots crossing at lower heights invariably land shorter in the court. Shots travelling 1 foot above the net reaching the baseline depths are frequently struck with uncontrolled force. The touring pros might be an exception to this testimony though at times their consistency is also affected.

Another underlying reason behind using elevated heights is that players utilize more distance than 78 feet from baseline to baseline. The elevation in the air above the net adds to the distance of travel. Even if the ball skims the net by 1 inch, the distance the ball travels from baseline to baseline will be geometrically greater than 78 feet. No matter how high or low the balls travel over the net, all shots display a curve and an arc. Each shot struck depends on the combination of heights, power and a player's *feel.*

You will discover the tennis court in those lofty heights situated above the net tape. Every type of shot that you could ever create has a particular place where it crosses the net. This action distinguishes where the ball will land. Therefore, chart the heights of your own shots. Observe where the ball lands according to the speeds and spins you create.

Nothing eliminates a player's limitations quicker than expanding the court that a player competes on. Many players greatly limit their abilities when they apply only 1 or 2 feet over the net with their aims. Players who focus on measurements of height and court space take an intuitive journey into their own creative potential.

DOUBLES POACHING

It must be said that a good doubles poach depends on players' bare athleticism. Some tennis players' strengths are indebted to their skillfulness and precision. Other tennis players' greatest strengths are their athletic features. Several players have the combination of both elements. Even if players never attempt to poach and have no intention to do so, a generous understanding of the nature of poaching highly informs them regarding what ensues in a match.

The poach focuses on the individualized ability of each doubles player combined with an awareness of the opponents aptitude. Learning about poaching will facilitate your reactions. You will also see into the mind of the poacher. You will observe how and why your opponents feint movements as they do and what to expect. Even if you never poach, you will benefit from this knowledge.

What denotes a doubles player who poaches? The tennis poacher positions at the net and then suddenly jumps out into the vicinity where the ball travels the majority of the time. A poach consists of player's determination mixed with calculation. Sometimes poachers make accidental winners. But decisions to poach are never accidental for the art of poaching is about the plan.

Aggressive poachers move rapidly through the tennis court, regardless of their hesitation. Poaching is beautiful due to the surprise element, the speedy footwork, the quick instinctive reaction and the express delivery. Doubles players who poach effectively analyze doubles differently than players who forego the style. A doubles poacher takes promising risks on the tennis court.

Some players believe when they notice a ball veering toward their doubles partner, they assume that they too have a chance to strike it so they step out in front of their doubles partner and make an attempt. These players innocently believe that this move constitutes good poaching. Their movements are ineffective because they lack the constitutional features of poaching. The decision to poach is created before the point has even begun. A player who waits near the net with a plan to fly into the middle of the court every time the ball flies across the tennis net represents a different grade of poacher.

The good poacher anticipates how the ball will stride through the court. This player has quickly developed a mental inventory about both opponents and predicts what to expect from their racquet strikes. This poacher is aware that 60% to 70% of the balls cross somewhere through the middle of the court. Retaining this information, the doubles poacher emerges in the same vicinity where the balls habitually cross. But the poacher should not depart at the precise moment when the ball crosses the net. An assertive doubles poacher observes and watches the racquet of the opponent, the ball's departure and will sense early what might transpire. Poachers who decide to strike the ball at that moment when the ball is already on their side (of the court) display a weak decision. The strong poacher resolves to poach before the opponent has struck the ball. Consequently, the poacher reads the opponent's racquet to get a forecast of the ball's departure, revealing the acute skill of poaching in the midst of a point.

Part 1: The First-Ball-Strike Poach

The most commanding poach struck is created from a return-of-serve. Why should this strike presume so much clout? Your doubles partner has just issued the strongest statistical shot of the match, the serve. If the ball returns, you, the poacher, are already near the net so you have the opportunity of a first-ball strike. Although not conventionally referred to as such, the volley that you hit immediately following your doubles partner's serve is a first-ball strike. Your poaching shot is the first ball that could go into the court and you want to make the most of it. Once the doubles rally begins and play ensues, the point can neutralize. When your doubles partner serves, the first ball that sails over the net can be taken advantage of *by you, the poacher*. This tactic displays imposing magnitude only when: 1) you are extremely athletic and 2) you can jump back to cover your side or your partner's side in a split second. If the poacher is unable to sprint to the ball and snap back into the original position, the poach shouldn't occur. However, poaching entails more complexity than this basic plan.

Part 2: Gathering Data

The preparation and the creation of the opportunity to poach is a team effort. It depends on where your team partner serves.

It also depends on what your doubles team has witnessed with your opponents' previous returns. By observing 3 or 4 returns, you receive a preview regarding *where* and *how* the returns will most naturally cross the net. As a doubles poacher, you are mentally gathering data pertaining to your opponent's style. You know that the returner has the options of striking alley shots, sharp angled cross-courts, lobs or middle shots. These shots are the balls you prepare to go after. Being alert to your opponents' aptitudes and developing the sense *on how and where their shots cross the net* is at the heart of anticipation. Ask yourself; "Where do my opponents most often strike their shots and in which general area?" When you surmise this data, your chances to poach effectively will thrive.

Your doubles team needs to perceive that each team member is responsible for 100% of the full court. In reality, your team shares the court and you both need this perceptive awareness. Each player is ready for 100% of the balls that cross the net. This delicate subject in competition depends on both players calculating what shall materialize as a team. Your team should be equipped with the inventory data on your opponents. You and your doubles partner need to be in sync with your shared information. You should both take opportunities to discuss your opponents' methods. Sometimes doubles players together may intuitively realize the facts necessary to know about their opponents. This advanced skill is shared anticipation. A player might notice an important feature about an opponent and alert the doubles partner. For example, you express to your doubles partner that you notice the opponent strikes a backhand easily down-the-line at a particular height over the net. Sharp doubles players learn to read their adversaries' styles like a book.

Part 3: Covering the Court

You have a definite advantage to poach if your doubles partner has a strong serve. After poaching, you must focus on your recovery after you have struck the ball or not struck the ball. You intend for your poach to never return. But chances are that it might return. Being unprepared for your poach to return subtracts from the effects which you have just created. This concept projects the one area where doubles players are often uncertain about their movement. Your team has 2 options: 1) to snap back into your original position like a rubber band or 2) to move into the area where your doubles partner originally positioned, given your doubles partner exchanges places with you at the same speed. Can you rely on your doubles partner to cover the area of the court that you have just left open? Can you recover and be ready on either side of the court in a flash whether or not you strike the volley?

Recovering from your poach at a *speed of light* is essential for a number of reasons. After you volley, you do not want to stand mere inches from the net. When players find themselves in close proximity to the net, little time is left to respond for their next shot. A spacious gaping hole is created between team players on the court because the poacher gets caught too close to the net. No matter how great the poach may be, if the poacher is too close to the net, the opponent's ball could return weakly yet the poacher has now lost the necessary balance to soundly strike, destroying the fine ploy just created.

Part 4: Aim

Where should the poacher aim? When the player races across the court and the ball moves at such a rapid rate, merely getting the racquet on the ball is more than satisfactory. The momentum of the poacher hustling across the court will add power to the shot. In the heat of the action, if the poacher can strike deep through the middle of the court or create sharp angles, that's a bonus. The theme of poaching should not be about rallying at the net and having volley sessions. If it occurs, players have to succumb to it. The intent is never to see how many volleys everyone strikes while at the net. Some players have the misconception that doubles is effectively played when everyone volleys within the same point. Although observing volley play may be exciting, volley-rallying is really neutralizing and should be avoided.

The evolution from 20th to 21st century tennis has transfigured strategic performance, leaving several players to encounter a blurred picture as they attempt to solve their doubles concerns. Not every doubles player is made to poach or charge the net. Players who understand the information about these mentioned skills (*The First-Ball-Strike Poach, Gathering Data, Covering the Court, Aim*) will instantly play stronger doubles games. Players capable of applying all of the skills will poach profitably. Players are better off not to attempt the poach if only a few elements are used. The shot is a real gamble and full of intricate design. Doubles players routinely charging the net are better equipped if they first learn poaching methods. Vehemently charging the net might intimidate some opponents but seasoned players (as you will soon become) are not distracted by opponents' facade. On the flip side of this picture, when you compete against the poachers, remain calm, composed and focused. You are now alert if and when your opponents' poaching is really successful. Your team now recognizes your poaching opponents too are on the lookout for particular shots which *you naturally strike*. As opponents do poach, your team will be ready. Nonetheless, you and your doubles partner are aware not to recreate scenarios inviting chances for your opponents' poaching to reoccur.

Poaching is a complex exchange which utilizes several thematic dimensions within seconds. Players foretell what opponents are capable of producing. Players process this information and act the moment that their opponents strike. The tactical design is a decision, a dance and an activity that relies on players being very fast. Lateral and backward movement is equally required for poaching instead of the lone, charge-the-net forward dash.

Although this explanatory sketch is applicable for the net player whose doubles partner serves, the poaching technique can be equally used during the flurry of a point. If you choose to utilize poaching methods, you should have a firm grasp of this section for your utmost success.

3

INTRODUCTION TO THE VISUAL APPROACH

A visual image imparts an instantaneous impression equivalent to a thousand-worded explanation. Spectators who utilize visual approaches enhance their games to their ultimate stratums. Today's visual technology has abundantly flooded the Internet with instructional imagery. Never in tennis history has such a bloom of opportunity existed for players who sincerely desire to improve. Televised tennis matches along with Internet videos and clips display the top touring tennis players in action. Overlooking this vast amount of visual information discounts the most effective teaching tools. The operational use of visual tennis imagery must be put into players' routines to gain the full latitude of physical techniques.

Televised players competing in the tennis Grand Slams (US Opens, Wimbledons, French Opens and Australian Opens) along with the other professional tournaments throughout the year are the finest visual instructional teachers that players can encounter. These players display an unsurpassed performance because literally these players are the best in the world. Since most players are looking to be efficacious on the court, it would be wise to examine and study the best.

World-touring players share similar paradigms regarding their groundstrokes, serves, volleys etc... Although the main prototype is repeated, an observer may find that the ascribed tennis features are never identical from one pro player to the next. Your questions should revolve around distinct themes as you watch these players in action. When specific criteria are pointed out to you, your comprehension is inevitably changed. This opposes a player who watches without proper guidance. Some tennis players feel that watching these pros perform is completely useless. Some players believe that there is a lack of connection existing between their own individualized manner and the pro's visual presentation. This theory is incorrect. When players perceive a lack of identification with the touring player's technique, this really shows that they are uninformed regarding the *detail they should focus on*. Once insight is gained, how and why these players move their hands, racquets and bodies in the presumed manner, players can easier alter their motions to comply with the style. No player consistently applies a tennis skill until it's understood, whether consciously or subliminally. Learning achieved through repeated muscle-memory activity is a method to develop seamless tennis skills and although this process takes a long time, guided observation regarding focal points is just as valuable, instantly speeding up learning skills.

The sections within this chapter, *The Visual Approach*, discuss themes and areas which players should examine when watching tennis. Before elaborating on televised observation, a short discussion about "live" competition is added. The chance to view "live" professional tennis tournaments is a luxury. The world-class tennis player displays qualities unrecognizable on the televised screen or video clips.

Topspin, slices, spins, flat shots, angles, one-handed and two-handed forehands and backhands with looping endings are attributes uniquely influenced by the court types and countries where these players lived. A player's strokes are influenced by body structure. Diversified body types favor some players to create particular shots which other professional players within their same performance level would struggle with.

If you have the chance to assay a "live" professional tennis match, you add power, agility and zest to your game. Observe how much court is utilized during live tennis. Observe the height of the ball's kick after landing near the baseline. Most strokes are struck with an open stance. Contrary to what might be predicted, these players strike many shots through the court's center. Notice how erect players' torsos are as they strike their shots. Notice how players elevate and literally jump into the air when striking the ball. Jumping upward, opposed to leaning forward, is more obvious in person. A player's weight propelled forward over a groundstroke is never beneficial like a player's body that stays upright and perhaps twists ad interim. The momentum of an upright body moving through the shot during impact is much different than a torso that leans forward. Propelling full weight forward on the groundstroke is out-dated. Notice the slow straight ascent from the touring player's service ball toss. Observe the deliberate motion of the tossing arm.

"Live" Observations

- How much court area is utilized by the player's movement and where the balls bounce

- The ball travel and the distance of the high-kicking bounce

- How upright a player's torso is when striking the ball

- How a player elevates and jumps when striking the ball

- The various types of open stance used by players

- The numerous balls which land near the center of the court

- The upright momentum of a player's body when moving forward

- How carefully the ball toss is placed

The next sections review technique that can be observed from televised tennis matches and Internet video segments. These references will instantly improve your game.

OPEN STANCE

Players exhibited an open stance only in those desolate moments when reaching for far-flung, distant bounces. Players were aware of the advantages but the standard rhetoric did not support or include instruction for the movement. Nevertheless, today all singles and doubles players should use open stance for added power and athletic freedom.

Open stance refers to the feet positioning and opening or facing of the torso toward the net. A variety of instructional approaches are available to teach the technique. Whether one form is better than another is entirely up to a player's personal judgment. Methods range from generating power from shifting hips to shifting weight (side-to-side) by managing the footwork. Ardent concerns on where and how to place the feet before a player arrives to the ball are superfluous and unnecessary. At times, the feet are semi-open, sometimes the shoulder turn is effective and sometimes the body rotates after the hips twist. Feet customarily point toward the net. Open stance fosters the ability for sudden motion allowing players to arrive sooner to the ball. The "turn" is no longer obligatory. Players spring out of the shot immediately after striking it, placing themselves in a perpetual ready position.

When you observe the open stance used by televised players, notice how frequently it occurs with groundstrokes and volleys. You will find the number of open stance shots is equal to and even outnumbers non-open stance shots in competition.

Ironically, introductory instruction rarely teaches players the open stance. However, as a player progresses in skill, the open stance is absolutely necessary for stronger recovery. All players ought to be taught the open stance from the beginning of their learning curve. Why would a player want to learn a limited restricted style over the natural athletic method? Players will eventually discover the dire necessity to use the open stance because of the ball speeds.

Do you wonder which type of open stance is best for your ball preparation? Every open stance is recommended. The descriptive pointers guide you to depict certain motions while observing the pros to later apply the same techniques to your game.

Coiling your body and catapulting from a turn generates power when a player strikes from an open stance. A tacit but relevant aspect regarding this technique is a player's vision beholding the court directly ahead. Since vision is the most vital element of *your game*, being in an open stance prevents your vision from shifting. Players observe the flight of the ball and the opponent's preparation simultaneously. As a result, a player in open stance is always ready to respond. For this sole reason, all doubles players should use the technique. The bonus from the open stance is that it prevents players from negligently striking shots into the net as their vision remains steady and constant. Paradoxically, you have probably been advised to avoid looking at the court while you compete, since the court is stationary. Nonetheless, you are in constant motion, facing the net and your vision is easily capturing your opponent's next ball strike on the other side of the court.

The open stance depends on the type of ball received. This explains why a tennis player's meticulous foot placement is secondary. Amidst the controversial lingo over which method is unsurpassed, the first requirement is getting oneself to the ball.

What matters is a player's strength. In other words, how quickly a player arrives to the ball with utmost balance is the goal. The open stance is dependent on a player's strength and generating power with the torso rather than being preoccupied over where to place the feet. Instruction is inundated with guidance on preparing for the open stance. However, players should really be engaged in strongly setting themselves up for a grounded finish. The open stance shifts weight from one weight-loaded leg to the other. This lateral shift of energy is very different from a forward transfer of weight. Shifting weight laterally from the outer leg to the inner leg or vice versa depends on a player's arrival time to the ball. Moreover, the open stance is about jumping, elevating upward, keeping a strong torso and keeping the chest open as twisting from side-to-side laterally shifts weight from one leg to another. Open stance promotes the throwing of the racquet across the body. Players should find balanced footing anywhere in the heat of the moment.

A player's sound balance can be indebted to the open stance. Players separating their feet feel stalwartly rooted on the court. If a player places the feet very close together, then tilts sideways, this player will fall unless the feet are quickly moved out of that flanked position. In contrast, if a player's feet are separated with space, someone could try to push the player over, but the player's physical orientation is structurally sound. The body is secure with a firm grasp on the court. This same principle applies to a player's physical structure when striking the ball. Obstinate balance sets up players to attain stronger finishes. Subsequently, the open stance is highly beneficial for beginning the groundstroke *and its ending*. A player's reactive strength for the proceeding shot comes from the cease of the last one. When players end their groundstrokes facing the net, they are prepared for the next shot with a clear view, straight ahead.

A particular forehand struck with open stance resembles the oscillating motion of an automobile's windshield wiper. Instead of the racquet-head moving around your body, the racquet-head shifts from one lateral side to the other. The face of the racquet remains parallel with the net during the swing.

Another forehand fashioned with an open stance occurs when players are moving. The racquet-head brushes vertically upward for the stroke's finish. The hand or racquet-head end above or behind the player's head on the same side where the ball was struck. These new evolutionary forehands rely on the open stance. The open stance can be used for every shot: backhands, return-of-serves, volleys, et cetera.

BOOST THE RACQUET-HEAD HIGH

Once upon a time, players were inadvertently advised to avoid placing the racquet-head high above their heads for a groundstroke. This tamed instruction directed players to swing "low to high" for every shot. The racquet-head was required to drop down underneath the ball. In days of looming topspins and less formidable equipment, "low to high" was the ultimate rhetoric. Balls found low to the ground still use this technique. However, the degree on how low the racquet-head should be and the *duration* the racquet-head must remain below the ball, these measures have considerably changed. When a ball sits high waiting for players to smash with a groundstroke, patterns of "low to high" as well as striking "over the top" of the ball both contend. Earlier versions engaged players to drop their racquet-heads lower than the hip for topspin and power. Those past patterns of low to high emphasized dropping the handle where a little loop was created with the hand prior to the strike or larger loops were created. The production rarely entailed to raise the racquet-head in space above players' heads. Racquet technology has conveniently added potency to the ball's speeds and the racquet-head emphasis is now placed above the ball rather than only underneath it.

Several incentives exist for boosting the racquet-head higher than one's head. When the hand is set high in the air, the hand is lighter and the palm can more easily dictate what the racquet-face will do. This method is dependent on the type of ball the player receives. If the bounce is high, the player opts to hit over the top of the ball. The shot is akin to a smashing groundstroke. If the bounce is low, a player may choose the low-to-high method. Variations regarding both aforementioned methods are combined to encompass all groundstrokes. Every stroke varies with former meticulous "low to high" maneuvers. Times have changed.

Watch how elevated the racquet-heads are on players' groundstrokes. Players boost their racquet heads for forehands and backhands (one-handed and two-handed). Pay attention to where the hand(s) begins and how it moves in relation to the torso. The hand is positioned in close proximity to the body and the racquet-head is pointed upward before it has been taken back. Once the racquet is taken further back, the racquet-head is placed much higher than the torso. The freedom and space players create with their preparation is a lift. The racquet-head carries authority over the ball when it stands upright, mirroring the hand(s).

Everyone should elevate the racquet-head for added power and control. You will gain instant power smashing the ball from up above. Tour players raise their racquet-heads to generate easy power. When the handle is elevated, the racquet is lighter in the hand for more precision. A handle tucked tightly below is limiting. Letting the racquet rip freely from up above is imposing.

The "high to low" method follows the pull of gravity. In opposition, when the racquet begins low and swings upward, the force somewhat fights the gravitational pull. The hand is easier to control when the arm is free and uses space moving downward. The hand and the wrist lead the groundstroke. Also, with racquet-heads elevated, players stand naturally upright.

This caters to a player's vision remaining level. Boosting the racquet-head is suitably assisted by the open stance as arms are free, open and extend with the extra space. Players who boost their racquet-head higher above their heads display natural technique. A player maintains definitive command over the ball, preventing the oncoming speed to dictate the power. This technique of striking over the top of the ball is supported by the open stance. A player's movement is accomplished with ease when the racquet-handle feels light. A raised handle invites a smooth stroking motion.

Boosting the Racquet-Head

With the racquet-head set higher than a player's head, the flow of the groundstroke becomes natural.

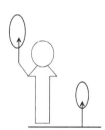

A player will gain great control and power with the racquet-handle upright in the hand.

Standing the racquet grip on the ground is similar to placing the handle upright in a player's hand.

Observe the *amount of time* players hold their racquets elevated before they strike. Lift your groundstrokes by raising the racquet-head higher than you are accustomed to. Leave your hand in the air longer than you have before. You will find sweet success by rolling your racquet-face above the ball, over the top and across your body. The technique of boosting the racquet-head can furthermore be applied to volleys, swinging volleys, slices and every shot that tennis players create.

Hands and Wrists

Tennis players rely on brisk movements of their hands and wrists. Players are likely familiar with comments such as; "That player has got great hands!" Hand dexterity depends on the agility of the hands. The fingers apply a certain amount of pressure also playing a generous role.

A player must first realize that the hand is dominant. The angle that the hand creates replicates into the racquet-face angle. Striking the ball with the racquet is akin to striking the ball with one's hand. Simplified hand skill is the best focus despite varied instructional technique. The gift is in the hands. The hand and racquet-face mirror one another hence players who pay close attention to the angles created by their hands improve their precision and *feel*.

Which aspects should you observe while watching these players compete? Which questions should you ask? Observe the player's hands alone by themselves. Divert your attention for a few moments from the swinging of the racquet and focus simply on the hands, one player at a time. Do the hands stay close to the body? How often are the hands near the player's waist level? Are the hands and fingers pointed downward or upward? Where are the hands situated when the players are sprinting for a ball? Notice how rapidly the hands pop back adjacent to the torso the second after the stroke is finished. Both hands return near the center of the torso immediately when the serve too is finished.

During the competition, you observe speedy movement and swings. It's absolutely pleasurable and effortless to watch a match without scrutinizing the details. However, to accurately understand what transpires, focus on the hands themselves, disregarding the actual match for a few moments.

The main counterpart to the hand is the wrist. Strength and agility echoed by the hands are amply dependent on the wrists. The hands via the wrists are centrifugal control centers since the hands specifically reflect the angle of the racquet-face. In the beginning and end of a groundstroke or volley, the hands return close to the center. On the run, the hands lift. Players must be aware of their hand positioning every moment to create agile and mindful-hand precision.

An Element of *Feel*

The Skill of the Racquet-Head Tilt

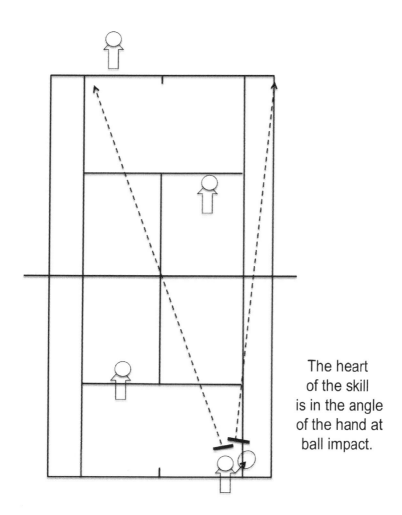

The heart
of the skill
is in the angle
of the hand at
ball impact.

A VARIETY OF ENDINGS

The end of a groundstroke is no longer consigned to one particular technique due to various ball speeds. The ending, notably the follow-through, has drastically changed. Players compensate for the best finishing maneuver they can muster in the moment. Forehands and two-handed backhands formerly concluded with the hands tucked tightly next to a player's ear. Today, this technique provides only one of many ways to end groundstrokes. Open stance and boosting the racquet higher are additional movements involved with these complementary changes. The innumerable endings are furthermore reflective of players' exquisite creativity.

Despite the array of finishes, rhythm and reason explain each groundstroke. You exceedingly benefit when you view all the styles displayed by tour players. These endings exemplify the assorted ways to conclude your forehands and backhands too. These finalized variations would have been highly disputed in the past for being incorrect. Every form is correct today and is utilized upon the demand of the occasion. It's vital for players to understand that one specific follow-through technique is no longer absolute. The descriptive examples present players with ending patterns to observe while watching televised tennis.

Finishing low, next to the hip and near the center of the body is the norm. This could be identified as an extreme finish when compared to the earlier conventional follow-through. The handle ends next to the hip or the racquet-head ends next to the hip. After finishing, the hand quickly slips to the center. This compact agreement of hand position and endings prepares players for the next strike in a blink because hardly any time exists between the groundstroke ending and the ready position. Hands cleave close to the body for quick, smooth and minimal motion.

One of the most modern finishes is the wrapping motion around the body. The handle ceases in the space between the hip and the shoulder. On variation, the racquet-head (instead of the handle) ends in this same place.

Another unusual follow-through imposed primarily with forehands produces a lasso-like motion above a player's head. The racquet nor the handle embrace across the body. This follow-through remains on the same side that the ball was hit from. The hand brushes the ball, lifting high above the head. When finished, the hand travels down the side near the center into ready position. This hooping forehand has heavy topspin. The hand and racquet whip above the player's head, producing sharp angles.

An atypical follow-through seen on occasion ceases with the hands in front of the body. This rather "unfinished" follow-through is all-inclusive. During these occasions, the hand(s) of the groundstroke stop in front of the body for more precision. Sometimes, after cessation, the player's hand(s) merge near the torso, cross over, drop near the hip and point downward. The hands then invariably move to a lower centrifugal position adjacent to the torso.

The oldest follow-through involved the hand or handle tucked behind the ear for a compact finale. Groundstrokes were once fastidiously struck in a straight line. The racquet-head tracked a straight horizontal line through space. The racquets did not wrap around a twisting torso because forehands of the past were mostly executed with a closed shoulder turn which remained closed after the ball was struck.

Advantageous Ways for Singles and Doubles Players to Finish their Groundstrokes:

- across the body

- lower than the hip

- over the side of the shoulder

- in-between the hip and the shoulder

- in a hoop above the head

- bunt out in front

- tuck near the ear

The moral concludes that a player's finish is adaptable and conforms to the demanding circumstances of the moment. With most of these examples, the hand/handle or racquet-head intermittently finish within a player's space. The comfortable follow-throughs are last minute adjustments for *feel*.

THE LOB AND THE FLOATER

Throughout this discourse the assorted usage of the lob and the floater is defined, compared and differentiated. The lob and the floater do not refer to the same shots. The lob takes on various characteristics where it might carry topspin, be struck flatly or hit as a chop high into the air. The floater is considered to travel lower than the lob yet it has similar features. Both lobs and floaters can be presented as aggressive or defensive ploys.

The lob and the floater are mentioned to denote their unfortunate and rare handling as offensive shots in professional tennis. You might view a player flip up a flattened lob when struggling to reach for a shot. That flat lob is often seen as a defensive shot from the result of aggressive play. A topspin lob or floater struck with heavy spin deep into the court was once extremely effective during a rally. But players strike with such power today, eliminating the possibility of topspin lobs thrown into rallies. If a player attempts to slow the point with a lob or a floater in the pros, it will be taken quickly out of the air by a swinging volley. This explains why the expertise of the topspin lob-floater combination has subsided from the tour. You may witness a topspin lob curve above a net player's head, however as groundstrokes and volleys have replicated into new forms, lobs and floaters with topspin are sadly fading from the tour's picture.

You may see a flat or topspin lob as a return-of-serve (mostly in doubles) or in the midst of a point. Although tour players typically lack the usage of the topspin lob and floater during a groundstroke rally, this shot is extremely effective for the recreational player. Putting tremendous amount of topspin on the ball is the first prerequisite for creating the topspin lob. Learning how to hit a topspin floater which sails approximately 8 to 10 feet over the net with a tremendous amount of "top" is invaluable. In order to properly strike this shot, a player needs to immobilize the oncoming power and "hold" the ball a tad longer to brush the ball upward. A topspin floater is extremely effective for players who intend to push their opponents back 5, 6 or 7 feet behind the baseline. Rarely witnessed today, the topspin floater is still very deceiving. Your opponents will watch the ball sail up high into the air. When your opponents finally realize that the ball will kick further than they anticipated, it will be too late for them to use offensive power on their stroke.

In doubles, topspin lobs and flat lobs used regularly for returning serve are effective when they cross over opponents' heads. Many players mistakenly believe that all lobs display powerlessness. However the lob is a shot of sheer, skilled *feel*. Using the lob is an advantage. Topspin lobs and floaters are difficult for opponents to compete against because opponents are likely unaccustomed to use the entire court space and area located above them. The utilization of topspin lobs or floaters insures opponents will need cumbersome effort to respond.

Instead of playing in a small, compressed area, enlarge and elongate the court with a topspin lob or floater. The ball will cross from one baseline to the other. The bounce of the topspin propels the ball up and further back than is comfortable for your opponents. This marvelous shot creates an obstacle for your opponents who attempt to strike with fluidity and power.

One final note: With the wind behind your back, topspin lobs and floaters work like a charm!

Topspin Floater

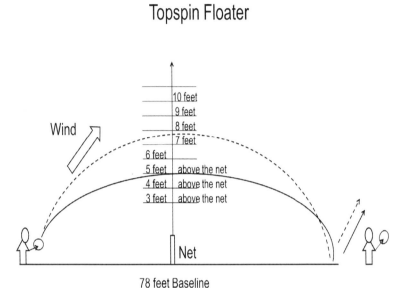

Wind

10 feet
9 feet
8 feet
7 feet
6 feet
5 feet above the net
4 feet above the net
3 feet above the net

Net

78 feet Baseline

The idea is to push your opponent
4, 5, 6 and 7 feet back
behind the baseline.

4

INTENSITY

While court etiquette and tennis accouterment have changed over the decades, the competitive quality remaining and necessary for success is intensity. Several interpretations epitomize what it means to play with this drive. Some players believe striking the ball with all of their might displays intensity. Other players assume that screaming and yelling at their self-made errors reveals profound intensity. But neither of these examples exudes the prerequisite required for an intense tennis player. Tennis intensity is passion, resolve, discipline, finesse and concentration entwined. Throwing tantrums every other point does not reveal high concentration. Striking the ball so it will never return exhibits power but lacks finesse.

Evidence of varying degrees of personal intensity are found in players' daily lives. That same intensity is typically displayed in competition. Levels of intensity players convey in practice are actually reflected in their matches. Wishful thinking assumes that some dormant fierce energy will emerge in the battle even if never witnessed before. The idea of applying the deepest concentration and mental intensity during competition is often overlooked. Players leniently using uncontrolled power may have led other players to believe that their crushing ball strokes reveal their intense demeanors. Playing tennis in this erratic, forcible manner is relatively undemanding, especially posed next to a player with a determined impassioned spirit.

Players who put forward resolute attempt each time that they step onto the tennis court build their mental toughness. Intensity encourages mental toughness and mental endurance. Players may never play an unblemished match since matches are never completely under their full control. But, players are capable of applying sound effort and discipline. In a lifetime, players may experience a few matches in the sensational zone, that universal concept which elucidates the athlete's ultimate competitive experience. Nevertheless, players should always strive to reach the zone's threshold.

Throughout competition, players need to know that their attempts to evoke intensity could wax and wane throughout a match. To prevent intensity from wandering, the competitor should bear in mind that each point is a new point and the last point really shouldn't be reminisced. Fantastic shots can be celebrated at the end of the match instead of during the midst of a game, breaking the concentrated effort. It takes courage to step up to the plate, to put oneself out there in competition with an intention to win. Everyone who steps on the court with focused intent ought to be admired for their attempts.

Competitive junior and adults should keep concentration constant before each point and throughout the contention of each game. In that interim, between the end of the last point and the beginning of the new point where that momentary lull exists, a mental break should be discouraged. Players allowing their thoughts to neutralize, giving themselves permission to lighten their attention, are misinformed. Players reviewing their last point played, celebrating or becoming critical in seconds, obliterate their intensity. Titillating thoughts derail a player's focus. Those free seconds between each point are opportunities for players to remain steadfast, alert and block out all thoughts but the next point.

Intensity is the most ubiquitous condition found in tennis champions. Consequently, competitive tennis players should be cognizant of their spirited choices regarding their personal court disposition. Acquiring tennis intensity should be initiated each time a player steps out onto the court. The rewards gained will continue to contribute integrity to a player's tennis game.

ECONOMICAL PERFORMANCE

Economical tennis focuses on the most efficient manner to control power. Hitting the ball with power is dynamic though the loss of control is a huge drawback. Players must weigh the advantages of power versus skill. Players must also ask how an economical performance can be applied to their tennis strategy. The tennis maxim once declared; "Put the ball into the court one more time than your opponent." This substantive theme is still functional but its premise is often overlooked because of the emergence of easy made winners. An abundance of power persuades players to believe that force surpasses consistency. Players must understand the staple principles of reliable tennis before imagining they win matches based solely on blunt force.

Competitive players benefit by doing drills and practicing consistency. Forming shots with touch and *feel* are tricky to produce with inbuilt racquet power. Consequently, the element of *feel* is often ignored as being essential. These touch skills teach players how their hands manage the racquet handle since the racquet-face is a mirror reflection of the hand's angle. Placing the ball delicately into the court is similar to placing the ball into the court with power when aiming at the same target. The difference between a powerfully struck shot and a more refined shot is indebted to strength, hand skill and the height above the net. A fast ball travels low over the net. The more refined struck shot uses varying heights over the net. Players must exercise both measurement skills to learn their potential.

200

Although the sport has evolved from consistency to powerful inconsistency, a player's consistency should never be underestimated. Not everyone is aware that the majority of touring pros who arrive new to the tour do not hit the tar out of the ball on every shot. Instead, they utilize consistency tactics blended with power. As their lifetime progresses on the tour, many players become quite familiarized with the games of their foreign competitors and the environment, gradually garnering the audacity to step up their power. The tour process steeps players' abilities, eventually molding players' games with more aggression.

No matter which epoch you learned to play in or which level you are, whether you play singles or doubles, the player (or team) who gets the ball into the court one more time than the opponent(s), wins. As a player, you can win a point from a winner you make that doesn't return. Or, you can win a point because your opponent makes an error. These examples are the only 2 possibilities to win points. This fact probes the core for winning any point. If you have opponents who can produce 48 brilliant winners in a row, then the match belongs to your phenomenal opponents. Realistically, how many people win matches by formulating 48 winners? Do players realize how many points will have to transpire to witness 48 winners? In all likelihood, those winning shots will be happily accompanied with an approximated doubled amount of errors - 98. This hypothetical example frames the reality of players who attempt to win strictly from winners. To focus on solely creating winners in practice is impractical since tennis matches are won with skill, intelligent strategy and power combined.

If you play an opponent who produces 2 winners per game, those 2 winners do not assure that your opponent wins that game. While generating 2 flashy winners, your opponent is still liable to lose every game played! 2 winners fashioned per game could help the opponent get ahead in the game, *but only under the condition when 2 to 4 errors didn't accompany them.*

You may lose 2 points due to your opponent's 2 winners. Yet, if you happened to place the ball in the court 4 more times than your opponent via the other 4 points, you win the game! The nature of tennis requires that players remain unruffled and hold tight during the suspense till the advantageous moments come around.

These scoring tactics are equally applicable to singles and doubles players. If you are a doubles player and your team makes 2 winners per game but loses the other 4 points within the same game, your team has simply recreated the scenario just mentioned. Rather than doubles teams being concerned with challenging and unreliable plays such as abandoning the baseline and rushing the net, randomly blocking volleys or formulating shots that they are unsure of, these teams are now mindful that they would be better off calculating the results. If each doubles team notes the number of points they win (per game) versus the gifts they charitably give away from their errors, they recognize tennis strategy at its purest. If the team identifies the fact that they are losing points from their own errors, they immediately have a chance to change their tactics.

Recall the underlying system of the serve and return-of-serve. Those initial starter shots, the serve and the return-of-serve, count greater than sheer groundstroke or volley winners.

If you strike a great serve and it rebounds weakly to your side, you command the point. You should be certain if you plan to create a first-ball strike winner, you make the shot. If you miss, it's regrettable because you are serving. That first-ball strike was prepared by your own serve or by your double partner's serve. Singles or doubles players should make fervent attempts not to error when depending on their own status of command. In fact, these mistakes are the types of tennis donations that you hope your opponents give to you.

Another obstacle related to power-hitting is the cost of true control. Speeding up the pace is perfectly fine. Except for when every shot is struck in the same manner, an intelligent opponent happily calculates the repetitive style. This astute player relaxes with the predictability of an opponent's repetitive mode, ready for the shots to uniformly stream across the net. Players who strive to take the top off of the ball, who strike the ball with the same mighty monotonous formula, do they realize that their tactic is common and foreseeable? Winners are never boring, however, shots missed "wide and out" due to a lack of control are disconcerting. Unforced errors are the Achilles heel of all players. Inner regions of the court and strike calculations should be impeccably measured. Players desiring to use their sensational power must become extraordinarily aware of the court space instead of assuming that they err because it's tangential ground. A player's first objective should be to take command of the power instead of allowing power to dominate and take control of the point. Players who recognize the select rewards of economical tennis will definitely win more tennis matches than they ever did before.

Playing Points Isn't the Same as Playing Matches

Keeping an ordinary vestige of 21 points where the first player who arrives to 21 points wins teaches nothing about the atemporal incongruity of a tennis match. Playing random points is less effective than competitive play (sets and match scoring) since the real pressure to win is missing. Playing points without a relationship to the appropriate tennis scoring is a waste of time. Players know deep in their subconscious that these points have little statistical worth. Points alone do not prep the player for the special type of tennis struggle experienced in sets and matches. A rhythmic tempo describes the makings of a game, set and match. The necessary competitive tempo is completely non-existent within the unconventional scoring. Since players' intuitions and instincts are significant during tennis competition, when players bypass proper scoring, they eliminate important components that influence the outcome of a real tennis match.

Players are called to bear down at certain scoring stages. Playing points fails to emphasize noteworthy moments that can completely change a match's outcome. Competition is never solely reliable on players' shot-making aptitudes. The contest is silently contoured with mental pressures of every sort. Players who play points without the confines of proper scoring reinforce the abandonment of their intensity.

Playing matches in scheduled practice sessions requires discipline. Playing points is more pleasant, lulling around freely on the court and repeatedly assembling shots in hopes that greater shots will appear after trial and error. Nevertheless, the more frequently tennis players practice being indifferent and lumbering, the more ungainly rewards will be. Those maladroit traits will emerge in competition when players least expect it. For example, learning to perform the serve-and-volley should be put into action during practice sets and matches instead of during random practice points. If a player is anxious to lose points on a newly learned serve-and-volley skill, that player will carry that hesitation every time the skill is put to the test, even though this player develops the serve-and-volley gift. Practicing the pressure of playing sets versus playing points lie at opposite ends. Tennis competition is about impending pressure.

What is pressure and what does pressure authentically express? A tennis player's self-expectation and self-judgment are linked to pressure. Fear of failure and strained with over-expectation place trepidation in players' way. Pressure is a combination of these qualities quantified at different degrees. Regardless where pressure stems from or its definition, playing in the thick of it requires courage, character and conviction. Pressure frequently claims a negative connotation. A player might choose to forego the use of the term "pressure" as an expression. A player might apply the theme of concentration to replace the woes of acknowledging "pressure." Concentration within the proper scoring of sets and matches obtains great consequence because the essence of pressure pushes players to higher levels.

Human beings would stop thriving without pressures, stress and the challenge. Without it people would let up and cease striving for dreams, goals and achievement. The same inference can be applied to every tennis player who competes. Perfection is an ideal on the tennis court and though never achieved point-to-point, the courage to pursue the perfection is revered. Earnest competitive players should pursue precision when playing their practice sets and matches and strive for perfection. Players should be extremely familiarized with the duration of a set, the endurance of a couple of sets and their patterns. Playing a practice set is akin to a mini-commitment sustained for approximately 30 to 40 minutes. What a player exhibits in practice is specifically what that player will display during the heat of the competitive moment.

THE SUPPLE TENNIS ATHLETE

Players' games might fall short of their expectations and the issue could be inconspicuously related to issues of flexibility. Perplexingly, many singles and doubles players who play tennis for exercise are less physically flexible than athletes from other sports. Perhaps the repetitive groundstrokes, serves and short sprints stiffen a player's movement. To become more limber, flexible exercise such as stretching may favor some players since haste activity is essential. The technological change has made yielding agility equally important to physical strength. Bending, swaying and the elasticity of swinging across the body are indicative of flexibility. Pliable strength requires that players jump, bounce and stay light. These physical movements have their origins in being malleable and strong.

Once upon a time, lifting heavy weights was proscribed because players believed weight work stiffened their physiques. Weight training has become a vital part of physical potency though perhaps lighter weight with more reps is still preferred. A sturdy torso is favorable to withstand the twisting during fast groundstroke endings. The additional twists that players create allow for racquet swinging alternatives. In this era of inventing shots, physical flexibility is at the core of a player's innovative strikes. The hands and wrists need agility since tennis players rely on their hands and its angles. Even a player's fingers need to be nimble. The head must stay steady to keep vision steady yet remain lithe. The shoulders should be pulled back to ensure that breathing is full and deep.

Every player is familiar with the knees needing to bend easily. A few players may return a ball found at their feet by squatting very low to the court where the knees touch the ground. This squatting movement may be more related to style and defensive play. By squatting, a player shrinks in height and goes against the progressive grain of lofty vision. An innovative movement displaying flexibility occurs with the serve when the posterior supporting leg kicks up after the serve is struck. Tremendous leg and hip flexibility is required for this powerful kick, granting the serve and body extra torque.

A player's attentiveness to become physically sinuous is suggested for those players who faithfully wish to exude more dynamism and creativity. The racquets virtually oblige players to focus on their physical regimens. As a bonus, being agile and flexible sidesteps injury.

5

HOW TO TEACH YOUNG CHILDREN TO PLAY TENNIS

(AGES 3 - 8)

The tennis world of a child is all-encompassing and must be guided accordingly. Implementing a first-class instructional approach promises that children shall be charmed by tennis throughout their lifetimes. Most children instantly experience an affinity with tennis. When children are introduced thoughtfully to the sport, they enjoy and prosper. A select group of children might resolve to strongly pursue tennis. Other children in the years to follow may compete and represent their high school team. When these children become adults, tennis will become a leisurely interest to share with friends. Tennis can be presented as decorum for family or social purposes. When children love tennis, their futures are filled with joyful childhood memories.

This section focuses on children ages 3 to 8, how to start youngsters and how to introduce them to tennis. Everyone recognizes that a child perceives the world differently than an adult. Nevertheless, this subject causes an occasional rift when adults attempt to guide children through the lens of an adult instead of considering the game through the lens of a child. Adults who embraced the sport when they were children have vivid memories of how tennis enchanted them. Tennis pros introduced to tennis at early ages were possibly impassioned by an intriguing element. Sharing the court with their friends, hopping, skipping and playing in the spacious atmosphere are sweet reminders of childhood pastime. Tennis under a beautiful blue sky and enraptured by the resonance of tennis balls being struck could also be recollections that adult players may have treasured.

Adults revel when they acknowledge success. However, a child measures success through experiences of happiness, emphasizing the importance of enjoyment above instruction. In the beginning, detailed technical tennis instruction is not the relevant requirement for major reasons. Children are situated comfortably near to the ground plus their racquets are small. The child's close proximity to the court combined with the easily manageable racquets naturally prime children's swings to be athletically correct from the start. The saddest scenario is when a child swings with elements of high quality yet not hitting the ball, unnecessary instruction is given that distracts the child from the naturally conducive swing. The best advice is to allow a child to strike balls everywhere and to move freely. A tad of instructional adjustment leads a child to have wonderful results.

Children have more formidable tennis athletic skills than adults imagine. Unquestionably, children should be introduced to tennis in the same manner as adults with the same court dimensions and rules. Adults should introduce many tennis concepts to a child over time which is preferable to issuing a droning quantity of only forehands in eager hopes that the child strikes 20 balls over the net successfully. The nature of the swing itself is the most important feature as opposed to the assumption that the ball must be struck in the center of the racquet strings. At the outset, children may not make contact with the ball, not with their attempted forehands, backhands, serves, overheads, etc... Regardless, demonstration is effective along with allowing the children to sample the range of possible swings. Praise children for each effort they make.

Teaching tennis to children comprises of two separate goals: the adult's goal versus the children's goal. Frequently, the adult's goal is for the child to strike the ball over the net and into the court. This goal reflects an adult's practical frame of mind. Children may not express it but they are also equipped with this same goal. Nevertheless, children have other worthy objectives too! Since children are accustomed to visually copy a model, when time allows they invent ways of their own. These self-inventions and self-creations on the tennis court are golden moments for a child. These attempts often improve children's tennis faster than direct instruction. Consequently, the main goal should be to commend children as they attempt to display what they have interpreted or seen.

Taking special inventive moments away from children and replacing them with adults' designs utterly dulls children's curiosity. Children should be allowed to stand inside the service boxes, on the service lines and in no man's land even if their heads and hats do not reach the height of the net. Children should swing from all corners of the court even if they miss every ball. You are indirectly teaching a child to understand the large breadth of tennis. One day these same children will strike the ball over the net better than could be imagined. Adults should play a few points, carrying out a mini-point or a mini-serve. The server sends this slow serve by standing inside no man's land or near the service line itself. The idea is to initiate real live play, establishing the impression in the child's mind. Children should be placed on the baseline and adults should stand on the other baseline and say something silly like "Hello" from far away. Children ought to experience a couple of tennis balls sailing toward them from one baseline to the other to capture the concept. The entire court is utilized by adult players so why shouldn't the entire court be available for children too? Interestingly, children innately understand this concept when the court or racquet they are given is different from the adult's version. To deny children the real sized court is to deny them the real game of tennis.

When children begin tennis, it's probable that they will miss when striking the ball and they may swing at the ball in the opposite direction. Parents will see their child race after the ball, catch up with the ball and take 3 or 4 swings after it bounces 3 or 4 times. Adults realize tennis is not played with 3 and 4 bounces and children know this too. Nonetheless, the value is in the child's happiness at swinging and chasing after the ball. An adult may become dissatisfied, especially if it's a parent upon seeing their child miss several swings and instead, watches their child invent creative maneuvers of their own. Unbeknownst to many people, *these creations have athletic and tennis roots related to the child's understanding of the game*. The key is that one day in the near future these children will marvelously strike the ball. Simply give children free reign and some extra time to adjust to the tennis atmosphere. Children will be overjoyed with the airy distance, playing in the expansiveness of the court. Children will be amazed at the realization that tennis is a game with many opportunities for creativity and freedom.

Adults should creatively explain to young children the classifications of the court. The baseline is at the base of the court, the alley is for a cat or dog they might have that walks up and down the alley and the mid line is situated in the middle of a few rectangles. Children need an embellished story to be delighted with the atmosphere. Building a children's world with real tennis terms creates a splendid environment. Children are smart and receptive and they should be taught accordingly. The conventional scoring (*Love, 15, 30, 40, Game*) should be taught to children despite their newness to tennis and their ability to strike or serve a ball into the court. A game with the word, *Love*, and big numbers that contain zeros is exhilarating to them. Contrary to what people may assume, children need and enjoy being challenged with unknown detail. Over time children should be allowed to perceive how much complexity exists in tennis. Spins such as topspin, under-spin and sidespin should be demonstrated. Diverse bounces should be explained. Adults perceive this creative approach as being too complicated for children, however, all children love the mystery of effects which they have never seen before.

Children love the trial of running after a ball that they attempted to swing at. This opposes the belief that children get discouraged quickly. Adults have the poignant capacity to get discouraged and again, children immediately sense when adults become dispirited at their inventive attempts. Colorful toys, yellow cones, poster boards and plastic items that stand large and wide on the court catch children's attention. Too, these vibrant items can be distracting. At heart, children want to believe that they participate in the same real tennis that adults play. Young children feel honored to partake in the real game of tennis.

Watching children hit the ball out of the court is perfectly customary because they are learning the space and the court's boundaries. Adults should sidestep a frown if a child strikes balls in the ballpark. The child is simply sensing an adjustment of power. Children naturally evaluate the court and they do not learn in a few strikes. The same can be said about adults. Children imbibe a lot of data in a short timeframe with a new palette of association. With an unconditional tennis atmosphere children will display their tennis abilities quickly, so adults must allow them the full range of freedom that they request and require.

It may take months, even years for children to recognize the complete strategic picture regarding the scoring, technique, movement and spin. Placing unnecessary pressure on a child's attention span is futile since children are naturally bequeathed with learning gifts. On occasion, a child who is just beginning may connect with the ball in the center of the racquet or even its edge. Outshining exclamations and admiration should be made. Adults should celebrate the child's attempt regardless of the result whether the child connects or completely misses the ball. The most unfortunate response a child receives is when an adult rewards only for the successful result. This response elucidates *one of the main reasons* that children decide it might be better to forego tennis. Most young children will absolutely love tennis from the beginning, even when they are innocently clueless about the sport. The color of the little tennis racquets, the florescent yellow balls that bounce and race off the white lines, a net that is at times taller than the children themselves and spans the court's width, the soaring space above, children notice all of these glorious features. How curious that children esteem the court's spaciousness, the area that has meaningful tennis significance.

Final Commentary:

Into the Swing of Things

The depths of instructional tennis formerly depended on individualized preference, diverse methods, instinct, athletic ability and talent. But the advent of recent technology and the abundance of televised tennis have led to realize that speed and force are the dominant factors that affect players' styles. Even if players choose not to use innovative power, the reality is that players will receive copious power from their opponents. Attempting to repeatedly produce flashy winners assumed as the norm by many competitors should really be referred to as, "tennis flash." The finalized results from those attempts actually lack the candid success that players want. Singles and doubles players are at times perplexed as to why those seemingly natural tactics are in vain for they may have been guided to play in such a manner. Trying to apply puzzling designs, players become stuck in the instructional jargon until they have their hands up into the air, asking why they are unable to succeed consistently. Consequently, players need a solid tennis structure to follow and a simplified tennis base that explains the mechanisms of power and advocates the winning percentages, which is what this book has intended to impart to its tennis reader.

A thorough review of your opponent's style is one of the best strategic ploys especially after you have developed those building blocks of your game, garnering tennis arsenal. The serve and return-of-serve are the main supporting platform for singles and doubles players followed by premier themes that have been acknowledged throughout the pages. Contemporary tennis has proved that speed and power control the game and it has made the effective tactics more obvious than ever before.

Few instructional tennis books are available by former tour professional players or today's world-touring pros. Players are occupied with a demanding career. I believe that many of the previous world-touring professionals have withheld writing instructional tennis books, recognizing the arduous demand to abridge their substantial tennis experience obtained throughout thousands of hours on the court, years of lifetime sacrifice, hard physical work, intuitive training and dynamic competition.

After decades of reflection, teaching and experience, I have composed the book that I wished had been placed in my hands when I played the tour. I wish that the tennis erudition and clarity had been profusely accessible as I am sure many others feel the same way. If the reader has any questions regarding the concepts I have written about or has comments to share, please email me at tennisstrategies@gmail.com

ABOUT THE AUTHOR:

Barbara Christine Bramblett (Barbie) is a former professional tennis player (WTA) who competed around the world in Grand Slams: US Opens, Wimbledons, French Opens (Roland Garros), Italian Opens, German Opens, Swiss Opens, Japan Opens, and all major professional tournaments on the Virginia Slims and Avon Futures tours in the early to mid 1980s. She was the first recipient of the honorable Karen Krantzcke Award in 1982, in Hampton Roads, Virginia. She holds 2 of the greatest tennis comebacks in world professional tennis history. In junior tennis, she won the prestigious International Orange Bowl in Miami, Florida, in Girls 16s, and the International Sugar Bowl in New Orleans, Louisiana, in Girls 18s in 1980, along with winning 75 other tournaments in Texas and within the United States in her younger years in both singles and doubles.

Barbie is a graduate of The University of Houston. She holds a Bachelor of Arts (B.A.) in History, an English minor, and a Master of Science (M.S.) in Instructional Technology from The

University of Houston Clear Lake. She has plans to pursue her Ph.D. studies in Information Science in the near future.

As an accomplished painter and artist, Barbie's oil landscapes, watercolor portraits and writings have been displayed in several art exhibitions; she has also taught painting for many years.